596383   C

D1559010

A REFERENCE GUIDE TO
Afro-American Publications and Editors
1827–1946

A REFERENCE GUIDE TO

Afro-American Publications and Editors

1827–1946

Vilma Raskin Potter

IOWA STATE UNIVERSITY PRESS / AMES

Vilma Raskin Potter, professor emeritus of English, taught at California State University, Los Angeles, for 31 years. She holds degrees from Brooklyn College (A.B.) and Duke University (M.A.).

© 1993 Iowa State University Press, Ames, Iowa 50010

♾ Printed on acid-free paper in the United States of America

First edition, 1993

Library of Congress Cataloging-in-Publication Data

Potter, Vilma Raskin.
    A reference guide to Afro-American publications and editors, 1827–1946 / Vilma
Raskin Potter. – 1st ed.
        p.   cm.
    Includes bibliographical references and indexes.
    ISBN 0-8138-0677-1
    1. Afro-American periodicals – Bibliography. 2. Brown, Warren Henry, 1905–
Checklist of Negro newspapers in the United States (1827–1946) – Indexes. I. Title.
Z6944.N39P63   1993
[PN4882.5]
015.73034′08996073 – dc20   91-17167

CONTENTS

PREFACE

This is a collection of indexes based on Warren Henry Brown's original alphabetical checklist of nearly five hundred Afro-American publications: Place-of-Publication, Year-of-Publication, Undated Publications, Editors. They make discovery possible, which always is the pleasure of scholarship. These indexes are preceded by an extended essay that suggests how the information in the lists can be related to features of American culture. The essay includes information on Brown, some of the early black women in journalism, what was printed in the black press, and an example of one major study of the Afro-American press based on quantifying work.

The indexes make possible wider use of the black press for direct or ancillary research in American history, black studies, American studies, women's studies, journalism, and popular culture. The scholar can enrich regional or period studies more easily with the directness of these indexes; all refer back to Brown's master alphabetical list, which is included here.

Scholars who address the enormous subject of black life and thought in the United States and who seek authentic voices inevitably will turn to the formative and enduring role of the press. Any master list of Afro-American publications will expand as scholars uncover more fragile documents of the past and attend to new, emerging voices.

Within the last two decades, black writers, scholars, and editors have moved away from, but not abandoned, the term "Negro" as either an adjective or a proper noun. There is not yet a consensus but a variety of choices: black, Black, Afro-American, African American. In 1966, Leroi Jones referred to "the Negro writer"; in 1968, as Baraka, he published *Black Fire.* Arna Bontemps and Langston Hughes, in 1970, compiled *Poetry of the Negro, 1746–1970.* Peplow and Davis used the term in their 1975 anthology, *The New Negro Renaissance,* as did John Hope Franklin, a major scholar, when writing a foreword for *Chant of Saints* (1979). Volume 41 of the *Dictionary of Literary Biography* is titled *Afro-American Poets,* but the essays use Black American, black American, and Afro-American.

ACKNOWLEDGMENTS

I am deeply grateful to the research staffs of the Henry E. Huntington Library, San Marino, California; the John F. Kennedy Library of California State University, Los Angeles; the New School for Social Research; and the Pasadena Public Library. I thank Professors Saralyn R. Daly, Eugene R. Fingerhut, and Paul M. Zall for their interest in and support of this project; B. L. P. for listening; and Lincoln University (Mo.) for their kind permission to reprint Warren H. Brown's pamphlet. I also appreciate the patience and keen eye of my editor, Lynne Bishop.

INTRODUCTION

IN 1946 Lincoln University School of Journalism (Jefferson City, Mo.) published Warren Henry Brown's *Checklist of Negro Newspapers in the United States (1827–1946)*. This thirty-seven-page pamphlet lists 467 daily and weekly newspapers; most are secular, although church publications are included. Brown found them distributed across most of the states; however, he found no black press in Arizona, Idaho, Maine, Montana, Nevada, New Hampshire, New Mexico, the Dakotas, Utah, Vermont, or Wyoming. Brown's plain alphabetical list included much useful information: names of institutions holding early copies, dates of first publication and suspension of publication, names of editors and publishers, addresses, and names of cities where the papers were first published, though not all information covers all the papers listed. He also included some name changes that show consolidation and change of ownership.

Brown's form is occasionally inconsistent. Where he found no expiration date for a publication, he sometimes used a question mark (?). Were the partially dated publications still active in 1946 when Brown completed the list? One cannot tell. Brown's spelling was not always correct; for example, spelling Charlestown for Charleston, South Carolina, and Augustus for Augusta, Georgia.

A weakness of the checklist lies in the identification of editors. Sometimes Brown gave an editor his full professional title, but not always, and other times he omitted famous editors: T. Thomas Fortune, Marcus Garvey, Adam Clayton Powell, the Pittsburgh Vanns, and others whom students of the Afro-American press will miss. Often he listed a publisher but not an editor; sometimes he identified both. In 1891, I. Garland Penn focussed on editors. His text included the engraved portraits of the young and middle-aged, serious Afro-American men and women whose work he respected. He believed these journalists were in the frontline of Afro-American advancement (Penn 1891/1968/1988). Sometimes Brown included the city in the newspaper's name, sometimes not. I have not altered his inconsistencies.

Brown's contribution is archival. Where can one find these primary resources? He identifies the institutions and the particular issues they hold. It is a heroic piece of work, but the alphabetical format limits its usefulness as a research tool; however, the four supplemental indexes should facilitate its use.

A REFERENCE GUIDE TO
Afro-American Publications and Editors
1827–1946

1

An Enduring Commitment

LIST MAKERS

Warren Henry Brown's checklist was neither the first nor even—by 1946—a complete list. Brown joined a group of intense investigators of the Afro-American press. Martin Delany listed the antebellum papers in 1852. J. T. Haley made a list in 1897 in his book, *Sparkling Gems of Race Knowledge.* George Gore, Jr. (1922, 14) added to Haley's list in his own monograph. In 1891, I. Garland Penn was especially interested in the post–Civil War explosion of the Afro-American press—in particular, the decade of 1880–1890. Armistead Pride, who became chairperson of journalism at Lincoln University (Jefferson City, Mo.), later reported the phenomenal growth of the press in 1902. Martin Dann (1971) added to Delany's list. Although Brown found 467 publications between 1827 and 1946, Armistead Pride found 575 in existence by 1890 (Wolseley 1971, 25). The actual count is hard to verify.

George Gore, Jr., while studying journalism at DePauw University, published a pamphlet, *Negro Journalism: An Essay on the History and Present Conditions of the Negro Press,* which included a list of newspapers and magazines still being published in 1922, organized by states. With some modesty, Gore spoke of his "mere outlining or suggesting of the field." He hoped to provide background for a better understanding of the state of the Afro-American press in 1922, to indicate the progress that had been made since 1827, and to forecast unlimited possibilities for an expanded Afro-American press because its appeal was "direct and racial." He was confident that the financial success of this press in 1922, in the big cities, meant work at "respectable salaries" (p. 25) for black journalists.

3

The brief main text divides his data historically: early, abolitionist, reconstruction, transition, modern. He further identifies dailies and magazines, adds a section on Negro schools and journalism courses, and concludes optimistically about opportunity for advancement in the field of journalism. Although the appendix of 211 publications is shorter than Brown's checklist, Gore's pamphlet is interesting. He shows how difficult it was to make a complete accounting of the black press: he repeats J. T. Haley's list of the leading Negro newspapers in 1897 but does not include all of them in his own pamphlet appendix. He finds more editors and some newspapers than Brown did in his list. In the first six sections, Gore attempts background detail, with some discussion of papers and brief comments on editors: William Calvin Chase of the *Washington Bee* "is noted for his bull-dog tenacity in exposing and attacking fraud"; Phillip Bell of the *San Francisco Elevator* "was well-versed in belles-lettres and dramatic criticism" (Gore 1922, 10–13). His model for these sketches was the work of I. Garland Penn.

Armistead Pride's massive list counts 2700 start-ups, of which only 175 survived in 1950 when his dissertation was completed. It was an outgrowth of the 1946 project of the American Council of Learned Societies' Committee on Negro Studies to locate, assemble, and micro-film this fragile record. Pride included religious magazines if they started as news dispensers and added the textual material, which is missing from the more austere Brown checklist, for individual newspapers.

NEW LISTS: WHEN? WHERE? WHO?

Warren Brown offered no explanation of his list beyond a brief prefatory paragraph. The sheer size of the checklist and its detail pro-voke questions from historians; from American studies, black studies, and women's studies researchers; from students of American popular culture; and from scholars of American journalism. Where did these newspapers emerge? Who were the editors? Did they work with more than one paper? How many papers existed before the Civil War? When did the greatest number come into existence? These questions are related to other varied phenomena such as education, literacy, population move-ment, risk capital, and personalities. Frederick Detweiler, studying the press in 1922, believed that the spread of these newspapers was part of a trend: more economic freedom, more restlessness, more adventure. But to play with such questions, one must have more than a mere alphabeti-cal list.

The Place-of-Publication Index of Brown's work shows population concentrations and suggests the gradual dispersal of Afro-Americans toward urban centers. The Year-of-Publication Index indicates antebellum centers of free blacks. The mass of publications confirms the growth of literacy and suggests the long, persistent passion to know more and to speak out on matters affecting Afro-Americans.

Almost half of Brown's list of newspapers (248) appeared in what had been the Confederate states plus Kentucky and Missouri. The antebellum picture was different: Brown found only one black newspaper in the South before the Civil War, the *New Orleans Daily Creole,* begun in 1857; two were published in Washington, D.C.; and nine others were published in New York, Massachusetts, Ohio, and Kansas. However, as a record of antebellum publications, Brown's checklist is incomplete. Martin Delany (1852) listed twenty-one newspapers in a lengthy footnote in *Condition, Elevation, Emigration and Destiny of the Colored People of the United States.* Most of these have not been found and this may explain Brown's omission. But Martin Dann offered a further list of twelve antebellum black papers that were not included by Delany. Of those, nine are missing from Brown's list (Dann 1971, 20).

Brown finds that during the Civil War five new papers appeared in the South and one in California. With a Year-of-Publication Index, we find them steadily emerging, year by year from 1862, decade by decade. Brown also reveals that these papers did not always last long; Gore doubts whether any early paper could have been a financial success, and Pride says they were prolific but not enduring. It is obvious that a public hunger for community expression needed a newspaper's voice: "At no time since 1827 has the Negro been without his own special news organ in this country" (Pride 1950, 403). In Huntsville, Alabama, for instance, from 1872–1923, there was a steady flow of newspapers coming into and going out of existence. In Atlanta, readers could find a black newspaper between 1891 and 1933 — not always the same paper, but a paper. Thirteen different cities in Virginia had a black newspaper from 1880 on. In 1862, an English-French black newspaper was published in New Orleans; the last black newspaper in Louisiana on Brown's checklist appeared in 1936.

The presence of free blacks in major northern cities and in New Orleans accounts for the earliest newspapers. At the 1790 census, there were 59,000 "free Negroes" in the United States; by 1830 there were 319,000 (Franklin 1947/1967, 217). To Brown's small antebellum group of newspapers, Franklin (p. 233) adds two, both from major cities: Martin Delany's the *Mystery* (Pittsburgh, 1843) and the *Mirror of the Times* (San Francisco, 1855).

Most of the 4,441,830 black Americans in 1860 had little access to schooling—only 488,000 were free—but in the years after the Civil War, there was a rise in literacy, which was reflected in and even confirmed by the quantitative expansion of the Afro-American press. In 1890, 57 percent of the 7,488,676 black Americans were illiterate. In 1910, the black population rose to 9,827,763 and illiteracy dropped to 30 percent. The 1920 census reported black illiteracy at 22.9 percent, and ten years later it was 16.3 percent.

Between 1854, the founding of Lincoln University (Pa.), and 1881, the founding of Tuskegee College (Ala.), thirteen more private colleges opened for blacks: Wilberforce (Ohio), Fisk (Tenn.), Meharry (Tenn.), Hampton (Va.), Virginia Union, Atlanta (Ga.), Morehouse (Ga.), Spelman (Ga.), Gammon Theological (Ga.), Straight (La.), New Orleans (now Dillard), Howard (Washington, D.C.), and Knoxville (Tenn.). After the 1862 Land Grant College Act, seventeen black land grant colleges gradually emerged. Literacy enlarged the readership of the black press. The Year-of-Publication Index identifies an explosion of black newspapers between 1880 and the turn of the century: 70 between 1880 and 1890; 117 more to 1900. To I. Garland Penn (1891/1968/1988; 115) the expansion of the Afro-American press affirmed "the triumphant progress of the race."

The expansion of literacy cut across genders. Men may have been the first and largest set of beneficiaries, but during the last twenty years of the century, women's lives and work were prominently featured in the black press. African American women journalists emerged.

AFRICAN AMERICAN WOMEN JOURNALISTS BY 1890

In 1891, I. Garland Penn, a twenty-four-year-old freeborn African American, published a compendium called *The Afro-American Press and Its Editors*. It included a laudatory Introduction (n.p.) by Daniel B. Williams, professor of Ancient Languages (Virginia Normal and Collegiate Institute).

Williams's validating sketch provides details that parallel the information that Penn himself accumulated for many women and men journalists he included: the poor, almost anonymous parents determined to

---

A version of the material on women journalists in Penn's work was presented as a paper for the American Literature Association, 1990.

see their children schooled; the lost continuity of studies; the brief teaching careers; the later return to schooling at a higher level; the still later newspaper careers. Williams writes that *The Afro-American Press and Its Editors* should be by "every fireside of Colored Americans of our country."

There is some evidence of Penn's wide readership. The striking phrase, "I am not coming to live on flowery beds of ease . . . ," in one of the letters to the *Chicago Defender* ("Letters") appears in Penn's chapter "The Anglo-Saxon Press" (p. 513):

> Let us remember that we are not to win the victory on flowery beds of ease, or be swift in running the race. Let us be patient until we shall en masse win the prize of education, morality, complete freedom, and citizenship.

Garland Penn's own Preface (n.p.) declares that the power of the African American press is to promote "truth, justice and equal rights for an oppressed people." And, the reader must appreciate "the scope and magnitude and beneficent results of its labors." At the end of his brief Preface, Penn apologizes to the hundreds of men and women laboring in journalism for not mentioning all the papers being published in 1891. "It would take ten volumes, yea, more, to make satisfactory personal mention in this work of the many laboring for the race and for humanity."

By the last decade of the century, the secular African American press rivaled the pulpit. Penn quotes the journalist/editor Gertrude (Mrs. N. F.) Mossell:

> That the press is intrenching on the power of the pulpit is growing more evident daily. People are coming to prefer to sit by their own cosy firesides and read sermons at their leisure, to traveling in inclement weather to the house of worship; and the poor feel they are thus on a level with the rich, or, at least, are not pained by the contrast in their conditions as they often are when assembled in the house of God (p. 487).

Penn believed the African American journalists had a moral as well as political task not separable from the broad needs of their people in the years after the Civil War.

The first seventeen chapters of Penn's two-part work describe selected newspapers, including the black dailies appearing between 1882 and 1891 in Illinois, Maryland, Georgia, and Tennessee. There were few such dailies, a fact also lamented by Mrs. Mossell. Penn observes dryly that "the prejudices existing prevent [the] connection with any united or Associated Press organization; which debars [the Afro-American editor] from the privilege of receiving telegraphic communications at the cheap rates accorded the members of such a body" (p. 127).

Penn cites another reason for few dailies—in the main the patronage of Afro-American dailies has been white, and to obtain and hold this patronage, the dailies could not be "too deeply colored" (p. 127). What did this mean? The black press reported prominently what the white press did not, or what the white press buried: the evidence of racial prejudice and insult by white institutions—police, hospitals, railroads. The black press reported white mob brutality directed against black men, their families, their private property, and their businesses. When their schools were inadequate and their urban neighborhoods singularly uncared for, where but to the editor of the black newspaper could African American indignation be carried? Who else was prepared to listen, or to act?

On the other hand, although black readers would be offended by a "neutral" black press, Penn found it ironic that two-thirds of literate African Americans supported white dailies and weeklies even though they cost more (p. 493). The African American writers and editors he interviewed for his book, both men and women, vigorously defended an independent African American press.

The major section of Penn's book (Part II) presents short biographies and portraits of the leading African American journalists, men and women. Penn provides the birthdates for most journalists. Were those born in slave states before 1863 necessarily the sons and daughters of slaves? For the group of women writers, he is specific only about a Mrs. Mathews. Sometimes he refers to their parents as "Mr. and Mrs." and sometimes he gives both their Christian and surnames, a subtlety that may well be code for "freed" or "born free." Some parents, like those of Ida B. Wells, were married both during slavery and again immediately at emancipation. Charlotte Forten approvingly reports the 1862 weddings of slaves newly emancipated when they came behind Union lines (1953/1981, 153).

Many journalists, when they were children, lost their fathers and, therefore, their first opportunity for education. Behind these men and women hover determined widowed mothers, some of whom are made visible to us in Susie King Taylor's Civil War "Reminiscences of my life in camp" (1902) (Taylor 1988). She reports how a black woman (Mrs. Woodhouse) taught a clandestine school for black children and adults. They sneaked into her house one at a time, hiding their books lest they be discovered "by whites or the police" (pp. 131ff.).

A singular feature of Penn's compendium is the self-validation of the individual writers. Penn does not control the text—he shares it.

Writers share with him information about other colleagues, they speak of their own ideas, and they provide self-portraits. Of the 140 portraits in Penn's text, 19 are women.

It has long been common for scholarly biography to embellish a life-as-text with illuminating reproductions of place, ancestors, self, and friends. Garland Penn's nineteenth-century African American journalists had become members of a middle-class group. Their markers of achievement were intellectual, economic, and esthetic. Earlier in the century and before, such a group would have affirmed themselves in oil portraits; later in the century they affirmed themselves in formal photography. Each writer in Penn's compendium is individualized in a portrait photograph, and each is real to Penn's black readers and white supporters. African American newspapers were created and sustained by the efforts of these people, whose serious faces convey an unmistakable impression of strength, energy, and will. One can imagine their voices.

Most of the women portrayed seem to be in their twenties and thirties. They present themselves in formal, dark dresses, and their hair is carefully arranged in late nineteenth-century fashion for urban, middle-class American women. They suggest what Joanne Braxton calls "exemplary models of black womanhood held up to public view" (Mossell 1988, xlii).

In a single chapter Penn introduced the Afro-American women journalists with flowery encomium: "There is a divine poetry in a life garlanded by the fragrant roses of triumph." Although they were all self-selecting for their writing skills, the women came from different worlds. Some had completed a college course: Josephine Turpin Washington graduated from Howard in 1886; Mrs. A. L. Tilghman was also a Howard graduate. Mrs. C. C. Stumm went to Berea, Alice McEwen to Fisk, Lucretia Coleman to Lawrence (Canada); Lavinia Sneed, Ione Wood, and Mary V. Cook all finished the course at State University of Louisville (Ky.).

Within this post–Civil War group of young women, most, but not all—not the bright Mary V. Cook, for example—came from upward-moving families. Poverty and deaths of parents interrupted the plans of others. Penn's "rose garland" embellishes the iron of their lives and their hard-won choices. Penn comments on Mary Cook's passion for study and her spelling prizes, which were the early predicting marks of later academic and professional successes. He refers to Lillian Lewis's "innate love of composition," to Georgia DeBaptiste's passion for education. DeBaptiste wrote to a friend, "I hope to become a writer of real power of mind and character" (p. 388). When still in their teens, Gertrude Bustill (Mrs. N. F. Mossell) and Ida B. Wells were both writing for what Penn called "our race journals." Women like Kate Chapman and Mrs. W. E. Mathews began their schooling late (Chapman at 12, Mathews even later after her slave mother's escape and long battle to recover her children). Mathews, who was forced to leave school when "her circumstances were of such an embarrassing nature," was largely self-taught.

Did the black women therefore bring more social and psychological maturity to the challenge of expression because many entered school later than white girls? As African Americans, did they move across a ground charged with the heat of serious moral and political discourse? Was not the newspaper an inevitable extension of their expressiveness? This is a group of women who chose journalism, chose to be a public voice. And these are women, writes Gertrude Mossell, who "trammeled by their past condition and its consequent poverty, combined with the blasting influence of caste prejudice . . . have yet made a fair showing" (Mossell 1894/1988, 9).

Mrs. Mathews, for example, was a "sub" for white papers in New York and then a special correspondent for African American papers. Penn calls her a "correspondent," a letter writer for whom newspapers would "dispense with their editorials to make room for her letters" (p. 376). Kate Chapman's career as a serious writer began as another such "correspondent." And indeed, "correspondents" were an important feature of early African American journalism. Readers engaged their newspaper editors and their journalists in elaborate discourse of public complaint and praise. Some "correspondents" beseeched editors for private help. Some, like Ida B. Wells, elaborated on their private experience of particular injustice in public position papers, which were widely copied (Wells-Barnett 1970, Chap. 2). This expressive relationship of readers, writers, and editors suggests that the nineteenth-century African American press was, at heart, a communal enterprise even though it was never sufficiently financially supported by African American communities.

It was inevitable that because these writers were women, some editors would assume that their journalistic focus ought to be related to women and children. Bishop Benjamin Lee, who introduces Gertrude Mossell's 1894 text, the *Work of the Afro-American Woman,* links the virtues of womanhood with racial uplift. And even Lucy W. Smith, who provided biographical information on women in the field to the professional publication the *Journalist,* also ran a children's column for the *American Baptist.* This particular journal, and another called *Our Women and Children,* also published articles by Lucretia Coleman, Georgia DeBaptiste, Ione Wood, Mrs. C. C. Stumm, and Mrs. N. F. Mossell. Mary Cook edited for the educational department. Hortense

Spillers refers to a female "corporate ideal," to exist "for the race, in its behalf, and in maternal relationship to its profoundest needs and wishes" (1987, 182). For an African American woman journalist in the late nineteenth century, this could mean being expected to cover women's issues, defined as child care, crafts, health, and nutrition. It could also include larger sociomoral matters: support of cultural institutions such as schools, churches, charities. The nineteenth-century African American women journalists seem to have turned what some might call a "limitation" into an opportunity to support, in particular, women's education and women's suffrage and to defend the race in general. Speaking of Mary Cook's "argumentative style," Penn quotes her outrage at the post-war abuse of African Americans:

> White faces seem to think it their heaven-born right to practice civil war on negroes, to the extent of blood-shed and death. They look upon the life of their brother in black as a bubble to be ' lown away at their pleasure. The same spirit that existed in the South 24 years ago is still recognized today. The negro is still clothed in swarthy skin, and he is still robbed of his rights as a citizen, made dear and fairly won to him by the death of those who fell in the late Rebellion. This outrage cannot endure. God still lives, and that which has been sown shall be reaped (p. 374).

Like Ida B. Wells, Mary Cook bore witness to the horrors of lynching in the United States. And like Wells, her voice combines the passion of oral discourse with her text.

Penn cites a second article in which Cook insisted that blacks unite and support black leaders. Many women journalists had observed, unhappily and critically, that African Americans were easily divided and difficult to lead. Gertrude Mossell linked this fault-finding, this "natural antipathy against our leaders" that Cook speaks of, to the failure of African Americans to support their press. The evidence that each paper reached a large group of additional readers and listeners was no compensation for the small number of subscribers. Nevertheless, to lose this press was unthinkable. Kate Chapman wrote to Penn, "Should we lose our free press, our republic would be shattered" (Penn 1891/1969/1988, 392).

As both writers and public speakers, these women journalists addressed two audiences. Penn reports on their public speeches, which were also published in the newspapers and, no doubt, read aloud wherever African Americans gathered. He provides a sense of the long tradition of written and oral exhortation, which runs from Maria Stewart in the eighteenth century through Frances Harper, Mary Cook, Alice McEwen, Lillian Lewis, Lucy Smith, Ida B. Wells, and Gertrude Mossell.

All of these women addressed audiences of men and women, blacks and whites. They were speakers at Baptist conventions and National Press conventions, and their papers were reprinted. The subjects addressed were temperance, women's rights, social justice, pious hypocrisy, education of women, women in journalism, women in public reform. Ida B. Wells's essays on lynching are still in print (Wells-Barnett 1987). Even Miss A. L. Tilghman, whose field was music (*The Musical Messenger*), urges in her opinion pieces, "Stand fairly and squarely for the race to which you belong, and whenever there comes a moment when principle and money clash, then stick to principle and let the money go . . ." (Penn 1891/1969/1988, 404).

What could their future be? No one could have predicted the enormous expansion of the black press. Mrs. Mossell believed/guessed that the literary future for African American women lay with journalism (she wrote for nine black journals). But at the same time, she felt that few women journalists were independent workers. Looking around her, Mossell judged that they were "satellites, revolving around the sun of masculine journalism. They still remain willing captives . . ." (p. 490). However, there were extraordinary exceptions. Penn cites T. T. Fortune, editor of the *New York Age,* who wrote of the astonishing Ida B. Wells ("Iola"), "one of the few of our women who handle a goose quill, with diamond point, as easily as any man in the newspaper work. If Iola were a man, she would be a humming independent in politics. She has plenty of nerve, and is as sharp as a steel trap" (p. 408). Fortune did not see her as a "humming independent." He never mentioned she was an editor. Nor does Garland Penn elaborate her experience as the editor of the *Free Speech and Headlight* (Memphis) 1889–1891.

When Gertrude Mossell spoke of independence for women journalists, she did not call for women in the chief editor's role. She wrote to Garland Penn:

> We have tact, quick perception, and can readily gain access to both sexes. . . . We are not in the thick of the battle. We have time to think, frame our purposes, and carry them into effect, unlike the editor harrassed with both literary and business work and other great responsibilities incident to such an enterprise (Penn 1891/1969/1988, 490).

And such exhausting, grinding tasks are exactly those described by Ida B. Wells in *Crusade for Justice.* As one-third owner and circulation editor for the *Free Speech and Headlight* (Memphis), Wells traveled, spoke, and sold subscriptions, all the while addressing race issues that were in the forefront — inferior schools and lynching. She could hardly be called a "satellite."

Lucy Wilmot Smith addressed the subject of "Women as journalists," and refuted Mossell's "satellite" metaphor. She spoke of male-female parity in African American journalism and offered an interesting comparison with white journalists:

> The educated negro woman occupies vantage ground over the Caucasian woman of America in that [the Caucasian woman] has had to contest with her brother every inch of the ground for recognition; the negro man, having had his sister by his side on plantations and in rice swamps, keeps her there, now that he moves in other spheres. . . . This is especially true of journalism. Doors are opened before we knock, and as well-equipped young women emerge from the class-room, the brotherhood of the race, men whose energies have been repressed and distorted by the interposition of circumstances, give them opportunities to prove themselves; and right well they are doing this, by voice and pen (Penn 1891/1969/1988, 380f.).

When Mrs. Mossell refined her thoughts in 1894, she wrote, "Our men are too much hampered by their contentions with their white brothers to afford to stop and fight their black sisters. So we slip in and glide along quietly" (Mossell 1894/1988, 100).

Alice McEwen, as associate editor of the *Baptist Leader,* read her paper "Women in Journalism" before the [1889] National Press Convention in Washington, D.C. She believed these African American women journalists would "mold" the national life. They were part of a tradition of "glorious workers."

> If we will nourish the seed sown by them, I believe we, in the near future, shall garner a glorious harvest, while women advance to a high moral and intellectual development. . . . All praise to these noble women. May their names ever live upon the lips of all true Americans (Penn 1891/ 1969/1988, 398ff.).

Penn tells us that she discusses at length the women whose work has been glorious. And this is in keeping with the Introduction in which he thanks the "great phalanx of our brave and ambitious women who have espoused the cause . . ." (p. 398).

Ida B. Wells at the 1889 National Press Convention read "Women in Journalism; or How I Would Edit." That year, she had bought her share in the *Free Speech and Headlight* of Memphis and was its editor for the next two years (Wells-Barnett 1987, 35).

Garland Penn found the work of these women journalists acknowledged in the African American press. In a September 1884 issue, the *American Baptist* gave an account of Lucretia Coleman's career. The *Indianapolis Freeman* featured articles on Coleman, Kate Chapman,

and Mrs. Mossell. The fifth anniversary issue of the *Detroit Plaindealer*
(May 1888) reported at length on the achievement of African American
women in newspaper life.

Women journalists were admitted to the Afro-American Press Association. Ida B. Wells was first the assistant secretary, then secretary of
the National Afro-American Press Convention meetings of 1888 and
1889. "No writer," wrote Penn, "the male fraternity not excepted, has
been more extensively quoted, none struck harder blows at the wrongs
and weakness of the race" (p. 408).

Though he praised Ida B. Wells, his respect, I think, was for Mrs.
Mossell. Wells had escaped the limitations of gender; Mossell's writings
seem not to have. Penn could not know how Wells's passion and intelli-
gence would carry her from Memphis to England on a long speaking
tour to expose American barbarism toward African Americans. Mossell
chose more temperate subjects spiced by irony. Her gender-issue papers,
"The Opposite Point of View," "A Lofty Study," "The Work of the
African American Woman," do not have the bite of Ida B. Wells. Mossell's public essay, "Caste in Universities," has the broadest point of view
and is a vigorous criticism of American racism. Yet, this attack is created
not out of her individual expression but out of a collection of quotations
from well-known African American men and from African American
newspapers.

Mossell appears twice in Garland Penn's compendium: once as a
journalist and a second time (with portrait) as an editor in chapter 23,
"The Afro-American Editor's Mission, by Eminent Journalists."

There are three editors in this chapter: T. T. Fortune (*New York
Age*) for the secular press, Rev. L. J. Coppin (*A.M.E. Church Review*)
for the religious press, and Mrs. Mossell representing "our women."
Penn includes their entire responses to each of four questions: (1) Do
you think the Press in the hands of the negro has been a success? (2) In
your judgment, what achievements have been the result of the work of
the Afro-American editor? (3) Do you think the Press has the proper
support on the part of the Afro-American? If not, to what do you
attribute the cause? (4) What future course do you think the Press might
take in promoting good among our people? In addition, Mrs. Mossell
was asked particularly to comment on the power of the press and our
women in journalism.

Fortune's metaphor for black editors was "servants of the people."
Coppin's metaphor was "the people's attorney." Mossell called the press
"a sleeping lion." Her reply to Penn was more practical than philosophical, and she appears to respond to a nineteenth-century gender expecta-
tion. Study other newspapers, she advised, and notice how they divide

their space among different interests. Study the constituency of the African American newspaper in any particular place. She was also concerned with marketing strategies to assure economic survival of the press. She advised to develop business tact. "Let the work and the field be studied, a policy marked out. . . . Form syndicates and pay for good articles . . . from our best writers and authors. Secure the assistance of some wise, helpful, intelligent and enthusiastic woman" (Penn 1891/1969/ 1988, 490).

Her advice to women (if they wanted it) who sought careers in journalism was equally practical: "acquire a good knowledge of the English language, and of others. . . . Be alive to obtain what is news and what will interest." Mrs. Mossell thought a woman journalist should devote herself to one subject for a particular journal until her reputation was made. She advised women writers to always use either their own names or a nom de plume. Many had already done this: Lillian Lewis was "Bert Islew," Mary E. Britton was "MEB," Ida B. Wells wrote as "Iola," Mary V. Cook was "Grace Ermine," Mrs. Mathews was "Victoria Earle." "Mrs. N. F. Mossell," if not a nom de plume, is a different mask. Married women journalists trod the narrow way between nineteenth-century approval and independent thought that might challenge male authority.

Finally, Penn includes her response that she believed "no brighter path opens before us, as a race, than that of the journalism of the present age" (p. 491). Mossell restated most of her advice to him in her 1894 the *Work of the Afro-American Woman,* but she left out the advice about the nom de plume.

In 1890, these women were certainly public optimists about gender equality in journalism and in black intellectual life. However, in 1897, the American Negro Academy would be founded for "men of African descent." Women's own intellectual efforts to improve the education of the young, the moral lives of the post-slavery generation, and their open attack on the horror of lynching was to be conventionally undervalued.

Now 100 years after I. Garland Penn's elaborate acknowledgment, only a small number of these women writers are known. In 1970, Ida B. Wells's autobiography, *Crusade for Justice,* was published. In 1989, a commemorative stamp honored her; she was also the subject of a 1990 P.B.S. video program. Oxford Press in 1988 published a collection of Gertrude Mossell's writings. And, in 1990, Frances S. Foster edited a reader of poetry and prose of Frances Harper, *A Brighter Coming Day,* demonstrating Harper's range of personal, political, moral, philosophical, and religious addresses and writings. The other intelligent, courageous women stand in the shadows waiting for scholars' attention.

Penn's compendium of African American journalists bears witness to an African American cultural tradition: to achieve literacy, to create one's own voice, and consequently, to create the audience—the listeners to this voice. The text (with Penn's own embellishments and flourishes) was created out of the voices of African American writers and editors. Penn sent out a call, and they responded.

READER EXPECTATION

What did the Afro-American press print? The events of the day and editorials; racial news that generally was left out of white newspapers; domestic matters, household and business advice; poetry.

Frederick Detweiler was interested in the poetry, and in Chapter 7, "Other Solutions of the Race Problem," he includes a small set of poems (1922). Henry LaBrie (1974, Chap. 5) speculates that poets who were published in the black press may have written "to attract an audience while feeling another way." He speaks of their dilemma as "the double thing" that continues "to shadow much of the black literature" (which appeared in the black press).

And they printed protest. The black press has had a long tradition of protest; they "resisted and argued strenuously" against the Black Codes of 1865. They printed "the daily instances of brutality and outrage that occurred—often in the face of their own destruction" (Dann 1971, 21). They printed amusing and angry cartoons. Detweiler found that in the cities, the black press was interested in "local improvements: better schools for Negroes, better attention to streets, fairer distribution of tax money for parks and other public facilities, efforts of colored people to be represented in jobs, especially jobs in stores run by white people in Negro communities" (1938, 396). George Gore, Jr., compared the Afro-American press to the rural American press in 1922: "The Negro paper has an unlimited field because of its personal relationship to its reader" (1922, 25). Pride believed that this press provided "otherwise neglected information that is the sine qua non of an enlightened electorate" (Pride 1950, 403).

And they printed letters. After the turn of the century, the Afro-American northern press—in particular the *Chicago Defender*—was transformed, in the imagination of eager southern black men and women, into a source of personal and economic advice. They wrote to editors as though they knew them personally. They asked: Shall I move North? Are there jobs for me? These are my skills; do you know about fair wages? I have been working around machinery. I have good references, references, references. "I am not coming to live on flowery beds of ease for I am a man who works. . . ." Their letters from just a short period, 1916–1918, were published in Carter Woodson's *Journal of Negro History.* Ordinary men and women, they are as full of political and sociological awareness as was Frederick Douglass.

Humble readers accepted the newspaper as their own voice. In his 1891 Preface, I. Garland Penn saluted black journalists who were "laboring for the race and for humanity." Detweiler believed that this press printed "the demands and interpretations of events that come to the surface in the minds of their people. Their atmosphere is one of questioning, discussing, talk in back yards, talk in the streets, in lodge meetings, in poolrooms; and sermons in churches. The newspaper editorial thus becomes the articulate voice of an inarticulate interest" (1938, 398). They were, as their letters show, alert to racial injustice and expected their newspapers to be no less. T. Thomas Fortune called the black press of the 1880s "a fighting machine" (Detweiler 1922/1968, 61). The catalogue of the 1986 Schomburg Center (N.Y.) exhibition, *Freedom's Journals: A History of the Black Press in New York State,* included a fine drawing from the *New York Age,* titled "The Afro-American Press": a group of nine black men and women stand solemnly before a long phonograph speaker. The text below says, "We complain all the time but do not back up the complaint with the sort of action that compels respect or reformation!" It is dated 1907. Years later, Roland Wolseley reported the 1969 story of two angry black men who were refused treatment at Maryland General Hospital and went directly to the offices of the *Afro-American* for redress of injustice (1971, 166).

The number of these newspapers—dailies and weeklies—does not reflect their full readership. In 1920, Robert Kerlin said, "These papers are read, and passed from hand to hand, and re-read until they are worn out" (1920/1968, ix). Detweiler tried to estimate the circulation of the Afro-American press in 1922. It was extremely difficult to reach and count them all. Sixteen years later he made an estimate of one million readers (Detweiler 1938, 394), including the humble and community leaders alike. The Department of Commerce reports in 1940 show the circulation of the Afro-American press to total more than 1,250,000. Horace Cayton and St. Clair Drake concluded that the *Chicago Defender,* with a circulation of 40,000, actually had a readership of at least 100,000. The wartime Office of War Information (OWI) estimated that four million black people read black newspapers each week (Finkle 1975, 54). Westbrook Pegler, who would have suppressed most of this press, believed they were "standard reading among colored men in the armed forces . . ." (Finkle 1975, 24). The potential influence of the black press at this time led to aggressive behavior. Pride reports that "hawkers and butchers [train peddlers] of Negro newspapers in the South have been the objects of mob violence, and even during the second World War, young peddlers of these sheets were occasionally forbidden access to army camps" (Pride 1950, 409).

WARREN HENRY BROWN
AND THE MATTER OF PROTEST

The black press has had a long tradition of criticizing many features of American life. In the early period, writes Roland Wolseley, "virtually everything was propaganda for a cause, a practise inherent in protest" (1971, 168). Maxwell Brooks conducted an elaborate study of the black press to discover whether the charges of subversion and sedition that Pegler (Scripps-Howard syndication) and Virginius Dabney (*Times Dispatch*, Richmond, Va.) had made were fair. (The black press was not alone in attacking racial policies of the United States at the outbreak of World War II.) Pegler denounced the press for "exploiting the war emergency as an opportunity to push the aspirations of the colored people" (Brooks 1959, 24). It was a charge Roy Wilkins of the *Amersterdam News* called "absurd." Even George Schuyler, the homegrown gadfly of the *Pittsburgh Courier,* recognized that the black press "challenged America's least reputable but most persistent 'way of life' so Pegler and his ilk want them suppressed" (Brooks 1959, 26).

Warren Brown was himself discomfitted by the aggressive tone of the black press. This may explain why he doesn't identify Marcus Garvey as the editor of *Negro World* and why he doesn't include Garvey's *Negro Times* in the checklist. Does this explain the omission of the Vanns (Robert Lee and subsequently his widow, Jessie) as editors of the *Pittsburgh Courier?* Or Adam Clayton Powell, Jr. of the *People's Voice?* Or C. F. Richardson of the *Houston Informer?*

In December 1942, the *Saturday Review of Literature* published "A Negro Looks at the Negro Press," Brown's attack on the black press in the United States. The article was reprinted by the *Reader's Digest* in January 1943 and by *Negro Digest* in February 1943. The titles were modified, and the content was only slightly edited. Brown was then Director of Negro Relations for the Council for Democracy (CFD), which Lee Finkle calls "a northern white liberal organization" (p. 73). The CFD was funded in 1940 by Henry R. Luce, of Time, Inc., to stimulate American enthusiasm for President Roosevelt's defense buildup. Its board members came from international business firms; some were editors of white southern newspapers. There had been only one black member, A. Philip Randolph, a labor leader and editor. Before December 7, 1941, the CFD had been one of the few white groups to pay any attention to the black role in the defense program. However, it took no position for better treatment of blacks in either the work force or the military.

Brown's article attacked "sensation mongering Negro leaders" and blamed communists for "the drive to embitter and unbalance [the Negro]" (1942, 5). He accused the black press of stressing race before Americanism and of publicizing matters that fed ill will. He grudgingly admitted injustice: "The Negro does not yet, everywhere in the United States, receive adequate justice." And he blamed the Negro press for emphasizing crime stories (1942, 6). The clashes in northern cities "are not wholly due to white prejudice . . . but to irresponsible Negro leadership," which aims "to capitalize on the war." Brown felt the black press "should not be encouraged" to hate-making, but he did not advocate muzzling the black press. He acknowledged the enormous black readership.

Warren Brown was one of the first to earn a Ph.D. degree from the New School for Social Research. In the Preface to his 1941 dissertation, "The Negro Press and Social Change 1860–1880," he notes the enormous difficulty of collecting materials. He quotes Carter Woodson's reply to his inquiry: that the Library of Congress and large libraries "do not preserve Negro newspapers even today." In the last chapter, "The Struggle for Social Justice," Brown identifies the causes the black press took up, even as he elaborates the abuses: they condemned court restrictions on jury service for Afro-Americans; they condemned the restriction of testimony by blacks against whites and the fact that "there was no police protection for Negroes against whites" (1941, 119). And, he identifies the aggressive action of this press as "based on the Declaration of Independence" (1941, 121). He offers a detailed analysis of the black southern press response to corruption, to class restrictions, and to political party manipulation of proportional representation at state political conventions. He quotes the *Athens Blade* (Ga.) of February 27, 1880: "We want good men to come to the front. Do not sleep on your rights!" (1941, 148). The dissertation also included a checklist of thirty-four weeklies (1827–1880) in the format he would enlarge for the 1946 list. Given the tone and point of view of the 1941 dissertation, it is hard to explain the 1942–1943 article.

Lee Finkle links wartime politics with the appearance of Brown's article (p. 75). Finkle traces pressure on President Roosevelt to indict "some black editors" for sedition, in order to curb the black press. Walter White, an ardent supporter of F.D.R., tried to use his influence to cool the black editors. The CFD believed it was charged to unify the country, hence, says Finkle, it "allowed Brown to write the article in hope of putting a damper on the black press" (p. 76). John Kirby, in his *Black Americans in the Roosevelt Era,* traces Eleanor Roosevelt's role in the Brown essay. In July 1942, she had agreed with Virginius Dabney's criticism of the militant black press; she found that militancy deeply disturbing. In January 1943, "in spite of her friend Walter White's strong dissent," she praised the Brown attack. John Kirby quotes her "Perhaps when the war is over . . ." attitude about opposing American segregation policies (Kirby 1980, 85).

Finkle takes a tough stand on Brown's essay. If Brown served F.D.R.'s political needs, he also served his own. Finkle believes Brown was a difficult and ambitious man who wanted to be the "Director of Negro Relations" in the CFD; after working for the council, he succeeded.

The reaction of the black press to Brown's article was severe. Finkle reports that the *Chicago Defender* started a "Bandanas for Brown" club.

In March 1943, Dr. Vishnu V. Oak of Wilberforce University answered Brown in the *Saturday Review of Literature* without naming him. He reminded Brown that the impatience of American Negroes is "desirable." And, he linked the domestic struggle to that of "all the non-whites in the world today." He asserted that the black press did in fact contribute to the preservation of democracy "by its virtuous fight in behalf of its people" (Oak 1943, 4). He identified the black press's demand for a new postwar social and economic order with the general assertions of the New Deal.

All this furor was in 1943. Based on information from the *New York Age* (30 Jan. and 6 Feb. 1943), Finkle says that Brown was deeply affected by the intensity of the response: "He avoided interviews as much as possible, and when finally cornered, he refused to give out much information except that he was very contrite and would try to atone for his past blunder" (Finkle, 77). He also believes that Brown's career in the civil rights movement was ruined. When Brown submitted a curriculum vitae many years later to *Who's Who in Black America* (1985), he omitted any reference to the time between his doctorate in 1941 and his appointment at City College of New York in 1947; nothing connects him to the civil rights movement. Publishing the *Checklist of Negro Newspapers in the United States 1827–1946* in 1946 may have been his act of atonement.

It is ironic that Brown's conservative attack on the Afro-American press repeats the themes — but not the style — of Nancy Cunard's comments in "Harlem Reviewed" from her 1934 work, *Negro, an Anthology.* There she attacks Harlem newspaper editors as "worse than black imperialist lackeys in foreign countries" (Cunard 1934, 72) because the Americans have some money and power. "They write vulgar, ignorant and abusive articles on Negro 'reds.' The Negro race has no worse enemy in America than its own press" (p. 74). But unlike Brown, Cunard called for a communist program to eliminate "artificially bred" American race hatred.

Though they were coming from different ends of a political spectrum, both Cunard and Brown preferred to modify the Afro-American press. But not the readership. In February 1943, *Negro Digest* polled readers about their feelings concerning the press. Overwhelmingly, they favored a militant policy and "were of the opinion that the black press had toned down the temper of the writings because of fear of censorship" (Finkle 1975, 77).

In 1922, Detweiler had been convinced that the black press embodied group life for Afro-Americans: "something like his church or lodge but even more like some public work of art symbolizing his aspiration" (Detweiler 1922, 204). In that press, individual credit became (by 1922) race credit, and once individual distress reached the newspaper, it became common race property (p. 197). Years later, John Gwaltney's informal interviews with black men and women led him to conclude that "there is an a priori assumption among Blacks that the prime preoccupation of social science ought to be race relations" (1980, xxix). This has been a prime theme from the beginning of the Afro-American press. How can this theme invite temperate responses?

A RESEARCH MODEL

The Year-of-Publication Index of Warren Brown's checklist shows that by the end of 1919, 317 black newspapers had been created and they had found their audiences. In 1920, Robert Kerlin published a small, detailed study, *The Voice of the Negro, 1919,* in which he traced the response of black publications to contemporary brutality everywhere in the United States in that dreadful year — the year of race riots in major cities. The Ku Klux Klan was an instrument of terror across the South and Southwest, and from June to the end of the year, twenty-five race riots stained American cities. James Weldon Johnson called that summer of 1919 "the red summer." In his chapter, "Democracy Escapes," John Hope Franklin chronicles the violence with icy restraint (1967).

Robert Kerlin, a white minister and a southerner, was a member of a Commission on Interracial Cooperation, which had been organized in 1919. When researching for *The Voice of the Negro,* Kerlin studied a wide range of publications, not all of which were newspapers. He included journals, magazines, and secular school and church periodicals. In Mississippi alone, he found eleven religious weeklies, eight school periodicals, two lodge papers, and nineteen newspapers, for a total of forty publications (Kerlin 1920/1968, ix). George Gore, Jr., listed seventeen newspapers for Mississippi; Warren Brown counted five.

Kerlin quotes from eighty publications, and for every article he chose as representative, he found at least ten others on the same theme; thirty-eight of the cited works were not on Brown's list. Kerlin's compilation of articles and excerpts from July 1 to November 1 was designed to show the intense attention paid by the Negro press to the great issues of 1919: riots and lynchings, the war, the discussion of the Treaty of Versailles, the Negro's "grievances and demands."

In his Introduction, he outlines his attitude and approach. He insists on paying attention to the black press for several reasons: first, because "the Negro has a right to be heard"; second, because "all classes of Negro periodicals contain articles on racial strife, outcries against wrongs and persecutions"; and third, because "the Negro press is now more powerful than the pulpit." To the editor who said that his book would make disagreeable reading, Kerlin replies in the Preface, "There are worse things than disagreeable reading" (p. v).

Kerlin includes a brief last chapter of poetry published in the black press. It is interesting that he includes Georgia Douglas Johnson's less well known public poetry: "The Question," "The Negro," "The Octoroon." He also includes Claude McKay's sonnet, "If We Must Die." All the poems express indignation and awareness of racial predicament.

CONCLUSION

Studies even more detailed than Kerlin's are now possible with these new research tools: Year-of-Publication Index, Place-of-Publication Index, Undated Publications Index, and Editors Index.

Roland Wolseley, a major student of the Afro-American press, identifies Warren Henry Brown as the author of the contentious essay in the *Saturday Review of Literature*. But Wolseley emphasizes the responses of both Oswald Garrison Villard and James Baldwin who in the 1940s saw the impossibility of a "Negro press without violence" (p. 306). What Brown deplored as being "race-conscious before being America-conscious," Villard, says Wolseley, saw differently. "These militant newspapers [wrote Villard] are both creators of the suddenly developed Negro sense of solidarity and themselves an index of a developing race consciousness and unwillingness to remain . . . a helotry in a democracy" (p. 306).

Wolseley himself, in 1971, is heartened that militancy in the black press is "not so much born of desperation as of occasional victories and possibilities of more to come" (p. 307).

Brown's master checklist was an attempt to create a complete archive of the Afro-American press. The final question researchers will ask is where can one find these primary resources? Brown tells us, and the names come from the Library of Congress through university libraries, antiquarian societies, state historical societies, state libraries, public libraries, departments of archive and history, and courthouses. The record of the Afro-American press is spread throughout the United States.

Scholars and curious researchers will continue to discover facts and to find uncollected dailies and weeklies, just as did Armistead Pride. In the *Messenger* (N.Y., July 1922, 438), a short editorial referred approvingly to *Ryan's Weekly* in Tacoma, Washington, and to the *Pittsburgh American*. In 1970, the autobiography of Ida B. Wells was published, in which her career as a journalist and as part owner of the *Memphis Free Speech and Headlight* is recorded. On September 5, 1988, the *Los Angeles Times* ran a feature article on the short-lived 1928–1929 weekly, *Flash,* published (and edited) by Fay M. Jackson (Part II, i). As the record of past publications enlarges, so will the inclusion of new publications expand the nuclear list.

Warren Brown would no doubt have preferred a dispassionate black press. But one is struck by the irony of his devotion despite his disapproval. His alphabetical list, now augmented by four new ways of seeing his data, opens this subject to extensive and intensive studies.

2

Checklist of Negro Newspapers in the United States (1827–1946)

Warren Brown did not always discover the closing publication date of a newspaper. Sometimes he included a precise opening date, but more often he used only the year. He left out the dates entirely on still other publications; perhaps he intended to complete the information at a later time. In 1947, however, he had begun an academic life at City College in New York, which in turn led him into a long career of public service, and he never altered the list.

NAME OF PAPER		DATE FOUNDED
The Advance	Alabama, Montgomery (Expired 1882) Issues on File: Dept. of Archives and History 9-11-80; 9-3-81	1877
*The Advance**	Delaware, Wilmington (Expired 1901) Issue on File: Wilmington Institute Free Library 9-22-00	1899
*The Advance**	Missouri, St. Louis	1882
*The Advance**	Rhode Island, Providence (Expired 11-14) Issue on File: Rhode Island Hist. Soc. 11-16-06	7-6-1906

Dates and spelling appear as they are presented in Brown's original, published list. The changes made in this publication are the listing in alphabetical order(*) by paper and state and the addition of information (in brackets) to regularize material.

*The Advance**	Virginia, Norfolk	1893
	(Expired 1894)	
The Advance Dispatch	Mississippi, Mound Bayou	1914
	(Expired 1933)	
	Issue on File: Duke University	
*The Advocate**	Florida, Jacksonville	1891
*The Advocate**	New York, Buffalo	1923
*The Advocate**	Oregon, Portland	3-1907
	(Expired 1933-?)	
	Issue on File: Oregon University	
	1924, 30, 33	
*Afro-American**	District of Columbia, Wash-ington	1892
	Publisher: Afro-American Pub-lishing Co., 1800 Eleventh St., NW.	
*Afro-American**	Maryland, Baltimore	1892
(1901–1916 as *Afro-Ameri-can Ledger*/semi-weekly)	Editor: Carl Murphy	
	Publisher: Afro-American Pub-lishing Co., 628 N. Eutaw St.	
	Issues on File: State Library of Massachusetts, Boston 1-18-30	
	Johns Hopkins University, Baltimore, Maryland 4-30; (1932) 5-21, 6-25, 7-9 to 7-15, 8-13, 9-3 to 9-17, 10-1, 12-24 to 12-31	
	Nebraska Historical Institute 7-08, 10-10, 3-25-11, 7-16	
	Fisk University 1933 (34)	
	YMCA Graduate School, Nashville, Tennessee (1929) 10-12, 10-19, 11-2, 11-16, 11-30, 12-21, (1930) 1-30, 2-30, 3-23, 9-13, 9-27, 12-6	
*Afro-American**	Minnesota, Minneapolis	5-27-1899
	(Expired 1905-?)	
	Issues on File: New York Hist. Soc. 1899, 11-17-00	
*Afro-American**	New Jersey, Newark	
	[Office of Publication:] 128 West St.	
*Afro-American**	Ohio, Cincinnati	1882
*Afro-American**	Pennsylvania, Philadelphia	1892
	Editor: Levi Jolley	
	Publishers: Afro-American Publishing Co., 704 S. Broad St.	

Afro-American *	Virginia, Richmond Editor: Obie McCollum Office of Publication: 504 N. Third St.	1939
Afro-American Citizen	South Carolina, Charleston (Expired 1900) Issue on file: Library of Congress 1-17-00	1899
Afro-American Mouthpiece	Georgia, Valdosta (Expired 1856) Editor: Rev. R. M. S. Taylor	1899
Afro-American Sentinel	Nebraska, Omaha (Expired 1911) Issues on File: Nebraska State Hist. Soc. (1896) 2-22, 4-25, 7-all (1899) 1-28, 2-4, 2-25, 3-25	1893
Afro Dispatch	Pennsylvania, Pittsburgh Office of Publication: 7611 Baxter St.	
Afro-Independent	Minnesota, St. Paul Issue on File: Minnesota Hist. Soc. 9-22-88	7-9-1888
Age	Georgia, Atlanta (Expired-?) Editor: W. A. Pledger	1898
Alabama Review	Alabama, Montgomery Office of Publication: 416 Seventeenth St. N.	
Alabama Tribune	Alabama, Montgomery [Office of Publication:] P.O Box 1624	
Albany Enterprise	New York, Albany	
The Alienated American	Ohio, Cleveland (Expired 1856) Editor: W. H. H. Day	1851
All About Us	Illinois, Chicago (Expired-?) Editor: T. P. Rawlings	1896
American Citizen	Kansas, Kansas City (Expired 1909) Issues on File: Kansas Hist. Soc., Topeka 7-26-89, 7-6-90, 2-20-91, 10-15-98, 4-00-03-05, 4-2-07, 12-15-98-00	1887
American Citizen	Kansas, Topeka (Expired 1889) Issues on File: Kansas Hist. Soc. 2-33-88 to 12-88	1888

American Citizen	Maryland, Baltimore Issue on File: American Anti- quarian Soc., Worcester, Massachusetts 4-19-79	8-1879
American Eagle	Missouri, St. Louis (Expired 1907) Issue on File: Missouri Histori- cal Soc. 12-17-05	1894
American Ethiopia	Virginia, Norfolk (Expired 1907-?) Editor: W. A. Conway	1903(?)
American Guide	Arkansas, Little Rock Issue on File: Library of Con- gress 1-27-00	1889
American Press	Alabama, Birmingham (Expired 1895) Editor: H. S. Doyle Publisher: Amer-Press Publish- ing Co.	1888
American Problem	Virginia, Hampton (Expired 1911)	1905
American Sentinel	Virginia, Petersburg (Expired 1881)	1880
Amsterdam News (Later: *Amsterdam Star News*—1941)	New York, New York Editor: C. B. Powell Publishers: Powell-Savory Corp., 2340 Eighth Ave. Issues on File: New York Public Library	1909
Appeal (United with *Northwestern Bulletin* to form *North- western Bulletin-Appeal*)	Illinois, Chicago (Expired 1923) Issues on File: New York Hist. Soc. 2-13, 7-18-85 (87 to 92), 4-17-97 to 1923	1885
Ardmore Sun (1901-07 as *Indian Territory Sun*)	Oklahoma, Ardmore (Expired 1911) Issues on File: Oklahoma Hist. Soc., Oklahoma City (04- 05)	1901
Argus	Alabama, Montgomery (Expired-?) Editors: Wm. F. Crockett and T. A. Curtis [Publisher:] Argus Publishing Company	1890
Arkansas Appreciator	Arkansas, Fort Smith (Expired-?) Editor: L. J. Van Pelt [Publisher:] Appreciator Pub- lishing Co.	1896

Arkansas Baptist Flashlight (Semi-monthly)	Arkansas, Fort Smith Editor: Rev. J. F. Neal, P.O. Box 873	1935
Arkansas Dispatch	Arkansas, Little Rock (Expired 1896) Issues on File: Hist. Soc., Topeka 9-30-83, 4-19-84 Rosenberg Library, Galveston, Texas 5-23-83	1880
Arkansas Freeman	Arkansas, Little Rock (Expired 1871) Issue on File: Western Reserve Hist. Soc., Cleveland	8-24-1869
Arkansas Herald	Arkansas, Little Rock (Expired-?) Editor: J. T. Bailey	1882
Arkansas State Press	Arkansas, Little Rock Editor & Publisher: L. C. Bates, 923 W. Ninth St.	1941
Arkansas Survey	Arkansas, Little Rock (Expired-?) Editor: P. Dorman	1923
Arkansas Survey-Journal	Arkansas, Little Rock Publisher: George W. Scott, 810 W. Ninth St.	1934
Arkansas World	Arkansas, Little Rock Editor & Publisher: A. G. Shields, Jr. Office of Publication: 907½ Gaines St.	1940
Associated Negro News	New York, New York [Office of Publication:] 322 West 125th St.	
Athens Blade	Georgia, Athens (Expired 1880) Issues on File: New York Public Library 10-31-79, 1-16-80, 2-6-80, 4-23-80	1879
Atlanta Age	Georgia, Atlanta (Expired 1908) Issue on File: Library of Congress 1-13-00	1898
Atlanta Daily World*	Georgia, Atlanta Editor: C. A. Scott Publisher: Estate of W. A. Scott Office of Publication: 210 Auburn Ave., N.E. Issues on File: Atlanta University 1931 Clark University 1933	1928

Atlanta Independent	Georgia, Atlanta [Office of Publication:] Odd Fellows Building	

Augusta Union	Georgia, Augusta
	    (Expired 1904)
	Issue on File: Library of Con-
	    gress 1-27-00
		1889

Avalanche	Iowa, Des Moines (Expired-?) Editor: A. S. Burnett	1891
Banner	North Carolina, Raleigh (Expired-?)	1881

Baptist Vanguard
  (Semi-monthly)
	Arkansas, Little Rock
	    Editor: U. S. Parr
		18__

Bay Cities Informer	California, Santa Monica Office of Publication: 1659 Sev- enteenth St.	

Birmingham Reporter	Alabama, Birmingham
	Issues on File: Dept. of Ar-
	    chives & Hist., Montgom-
	    ery 15, 18, 20, 28, 1-34
		1902

Birmingham Review	Alabama, Birmingham
	Editor & Publisher: Robert
	    Durr
	Office of Publication: 1622
	    Fourth Ave., North
		1933

Birmingham World
  (Semi-weekly)
	Alabama, Birmingham
	Editor: Emory O. Jackson
	Publisher: Scott Newspaper
	    Syndicate Publishing Com-
	    pany, 312 N. Seventeenth
	    St.
		1931

Black Dispatch	Oklahoma, Oklahoma City
	Editor: Roscoe Dunjee, 324 E.
	    2nd St.
	Issues on File: Oklahoma Hist.
	    Soc., Oklahoma City 16,
	    17
		1915

Black Republican	Louisiana, New Orleans
	    (Expired-?)
	Issues on File: Boston Athenae-
	    um, Boston 4-15-29, (1865)
	    5-13-20
	American Antiquarian Soc.,
	    Worcester, Massachu-
	    setts 4-22-65
		4-15-1865

Blade	Georgia, Eatonton (Expired-?) Editor: E. W. Lowe	1894
Boston Courant	Massachusetts, Boston Editor: J. Gordon Street Issue on File: Library of Con- gress 1-6-00	1890

*Broadax**	Illinois, Chicago (Expired 1919) Issue on File: Library of Congress 1-27-00	1899
Broad Axe	Pennsylvania, Pittsburgh (Expired-?) Editors & Publishers: G. A. Neal & F. Clark	1896
Brotherhood	Mississippi, Natchez [Publisher:] Brotherhood Publishing Co.	1887
Buckeye Review	Ohio, Youngstown	1938
Buffalo Broadcaster	New York, Buffalo [Office of Publication:] 168 Clinton St.	
Buffalo Criterion	New York, Buffalo [Office of Publication:] 367 William St.	1934
Buffalo Spokesman	New York, Buffalo	
Buffalo Star	New York, Buffalo [Office of Publication:] 234 Broadway	1932
Bulletin	Kentucky, Louisville (Expired-?) Issue on File: Yale University 9-24-81	1879
Bystander (Title varies—*Iowa Bystander, Iowa State Bystander*)	Iowa, Des Moines Issues on File: Hist. Memorial & Art Dept. of Iowa, Des Moines 11-96	1894
The Cairo Gazette (Daily)	Illinois, Cairo (Expired 10-82) Owner: W. S. Scott	4-23-1882
California Eagle	California, Los Angeles Editor: Charlotta A. Bass Issues on File: Public Library, Los Angeles 12-23-27 Los Angeles Museum [LIB.] Los Angeles 9-5-03, 12-15-06 Bancroft Library, University of California, Berkeley (1914) 1-31; 6-30, 8-22; 11-19; 1921; 3-22; 2-14-24; (1926) 1-1, 1-8, 5-7; (1927) 2-4, 2-11, 10-14, 12-23; (1928) 6-22, 7-13; (1929) 2-22, 3-8, 3-15, 4-5, 5-3, 9-27, 10-4, 11-14-21; 1923	4-8-1879

California Voice	California, Oakland	1919
	Issues on File: Bancroft Library, University of California, Berkeley 10-1-21, 1-7-22; 1925; 4-6-26; (1927) 3-4, 5-6; (1929) 1-25, 2-15; (1930) 4-18; 5-23, 7-4	
Call	Kansas, Topeka	1891
	(Expired-?)	
	Editor & Publisher: W. M. Pope	
Call	Missouri, Kansas City	1919
	Editor: C. A. Franklin	
	Office of Publication: Kansas City Call Co., 1715 E. Eighteenth St.	
Cambridge Mirror	Massachusetts, Cambridge	1906
	(Expired 1909)	
	Issue on File: Widener Library of Harvard 4-25-06	
Cape Fear Journal	North Carolina, Wilmington	
	[Office of Publication:] 412 S. Seventh St.	
Capitol	New York, Albany	1894
	(Expired-?)	
	Editor: W. H. Johnson	
	Publisher: Edward Abrams, 27 Maiden Lane	
Caret	Virginia, Newport News	1895
	(Expired-?)	
	Editor: C. D. Cooley	
Carolina Enterprise	North Carolina, Goldsboro	1881
	Editor: C. D. Cooley	
Carolina Times	North Carolina, Durham	
	(Expired-?)	
	Office of Publication: 117 Peabody St.	
Carolina Tribune	North Carolina, Raleigh	1926
	Office of Publication: 115 E. Hargett St.	
Carolinian	North Carolina, Raleigh	1920
	Publisher: P. R. Jervay, 118 E. Hargett St.	
Charlestown Journal	South Carolina, Charlestown	1866
	(Expired-?)	
	Editiors: B. F. Randolph & E. S. Adams Sones	
	Issues on File: Widener Library of Harvard 1866, 10-4-11	

Charlotte Post	North Carolina, Charlotte	
	Office of Publication: 624 E. Second St.	
Chicago Bee	Illinois, Chicago	1909
	[Office of Publication:] 3655 S. State St.	
Chicago Defender	Illinois, Chicago	1905
	[Office of Publication:] 3435 Indiana Ave.	
	Issues on File: Free Library of Philadelphia 12-30-33; 1-6-34	
Chicago Whip	Illinois, Chicago	1919
	(Expired 1932)	
	Issues on File: Chicago Hist. Soc., Chicago 6-24-1919-22	
Chicago World	Illinois, Chicago	1900
	(Expired-?)	
	[Office of Publication:] 118 E. Thirty-fifth St.	
	Issue on File: Library of Congress 1-27-00	
Christian Advocate	Missouri, Kansas City	
	[Office of Publication:] 1121 McGee St.	
Chronicle	Massachusetts, Boston	1916
	Editor: Alfred Haughton	
	Office of Publication: Square Deal–Boston Chronicle Co., Inc., 794 Tremont	
Chronometer	Georgia, Americus	1898
	(Expired-?)	
	Editor & Publisher: Rev. S. T. Hawkins	
Church Organ	Illinois, Chicago	1893
City Times	Texas, Galveston	1898
	(Expired 1930)	
	Issues on File: Rosenberg Library, 9-29-00, 6-4-27; Texas University, Austin, 6-11-04 to 10-14-05	
Clarion	Texas, Waco	1921
	(Expired-?)	
	Editor & Publisher: Allie W. Jackson	
Cleveland Advocate	Ohio, Cleveland	1914
	(Expired 1923)	
	Issues on File: Ohio State Archives & Hist. Soc. 6-17 to 12-18; 1920	

Cleveland Call and Post	Ohio, Cleveland Editor: Wm. O. Walker Publishers: P. & W. Publishing Co., 2319 E. Fifty-fifth St.	2-22-1921
Cleveland Guide	Ohio, Cleveland Editor: E. F. Cheeks, 2279 E. Ninetieth St.	1931
Cleveland Herald	Ohio, Cleveland Editor: O. A. Forte, E. Seventy- first St. and Central Ave.	1938
Clipper	Georgia, Athens (Expired-?) Editor & Publisher: S. B. Davis	1888
Clipper	Illinois, Chicago (Expired-?) Editor & Publisher: Cornelius Lenox, 182 W. Jackson St.	1885
Color	West Virginia, Charleston	1943
Colorado Statesman	Colorado, Denver Issues on File: Colorado State Hist. Soc., Denver 1-04, 10-27-04 Library of Congress 1-27-00	1894
Colored Alabamian	Alabama, Tuscaloosa (Expired 1916) Issues on File: Dept. of Ar- chives & History, Mont- gomery 10-07 to 1-16 Tuscaloosa Chronicle, Dept. of Archives and History, Montgomery 12-17-98 to 1-99; 2-1-99, 2-18-99 Tuscaloosa County Court House 1896 and 1898	1907
Colored American	District of Columbia, Wash- ington (Expired 1904) Issues on File: Library of Con- gress 3-12-98, 11-12-04	1893
Colored American	Georgia, Augustus (Expired-?) [Issues on File:] Library of Con- gress 12-21-65 Boston Athenaeum 12-30-65, 1-6-66 American Antiquarian Soc., Worcester, Massachu- setts 12-30-65 New York Hist. Soc. 1-13-66	12-16-1865

Colored American (Also *Weekly Advocate*)	New York, New York (Expired 1842) Issues on File: Connecticut State Library, Hartford 1-29-39, 4-29-40, 10-24-40, 3-13-41, 3-18-41 Yale University, New Haven 1-19-39 Library of Congress 3-37; (1837) 4-1, 4-15, 4-22; 9-29-38, 10-38, 3-30-39, 4-15-40 Public Library of Boston 3-37 New York State Library, Albany 3-18-37 Cornell University Library, Ithaca, 3-37 to 11-23-39 New York Public Library 11-17-38 New York Hist. Soc. 2-18-37-38 Union College, Schenectady 12-4-41	1837
Colored American	Texas, Galveston (Expired 1925) Issue on File: Rosenberg Library 11-20-20	1920
Colored Citizen	Florida, Pensacola (Expired-?) Editor & Publisher: F. E. Washington, 203 S. Boyston St.	1912
Colored Citizen (Followed by *Topeka Tribune*)	Kansas, Topeka (Expired 1900) Issues on File: Kansas Hist. Soc., 4-19-78; 1-10-80; 6-17-97; 11-16-00	1878
Colored Citizen	Kansas, Wichita (Expired 1904) Issues on File: Kansas Hist. Soc., Topeka 2-21-03 to 2-6-04	1902
Colored Citizen	Ohio, Cincinnati (Expired 1869) Issues on File: American Antiquarian Soc., Worcester, Massachusetts 3-19-66	1863
The Colored Man's Journal	New York, New York (Expired 1856) Publisher: Louis M. Putnam	1851
Colored Patriot	Kansas, Topeka (Expired-?) Issues on File: Kansas Hist. Soc. 4-20-82; 6-22-82	1882

Colored Tennessean	Tennessee, Nashville	3-24-1866
	(Expired 7-18-67)	
	Issues on File: Boston Athenae-	
	um Soc. 3-24-66; 7-18-67	
Colored World	Indiana, Indianapolis	1883
	(Expired-?)	
Columbus Messenger	Ohio, Columbus	1887
	(Expired-?)	
	Editor: B. T. Harvey	
Columbus Voice	Ohio, Columbus	1883
	(Expired-?)	
	Office of Publication: 385	
	Woodland Ave.	
Commoner	District of Columbia, Wash-	1875
	ington	
	(Expired-?)	
	Editor: George N. Williams	
Conservator	Illinois, Chicago	1878
	(Expired-?)	
	Publisher: F. L. Barnett	
Contributor	Missouri, St. Louis	1883
	(Expired-?)	
Courier	Indiana, Indianapolis	1893
	(Expired-?)	
	Publisher: Charles Stewart	
Criterion	California, Los Angeles	1942
	Editor: Jeanne Severns	
	Publisher: Arnold Scott, 124 W.	
	Sixth St.	
Crusader	Maryland, Baltimore	1893
	(Expired-?)	
	Editor & Publisher: Joseph	
	Dorsey	
Crusader	Pennsylvania, Pittsburgh	
	[Office of Publication:] 532	
	Provus St.	
Crystal	Arkansas, Hot Springs	1898
	(Expired-?)	
	Editor: J. R. Bennett	
Daily Bulletin	Ohio, Dayton	1941
Daily Express	Ohio, Dayton	1942
Daily Search Light	Oklahoma, Muskogee	1905
	(Expired 1906)	
	Issue on File: Oklahoma Hist.	
	Soc., Oklahoma City, 1905	
Dallas Express	Texas, Dallas	1893
	(Expired 1894)	
	Issues on File: Library of Con-	
	gress 1-13-00	
	Texas University 1919 to 1928	

Dayton Forum	Ohio, Dayton	5-16-1913
	Issues on File: Ohio State Archives & Hist. Soc., Columbus, 6-18 to 10-24-19	
Defender	Pennsylvania, Philadelphia	1897
	(Expired-?)	
	Editor: H. C. C. Astwood	
	Publisher: George A. Astwood	
Defender	Tennessee, Chattanooga	1917
	(Expired-?)	
	Editor: J. J. J. Oldfield	
	Publisher: Chattanooga Defender Publishing Company, Inc., 750 Twenty-ninth St.	
Delaware Twilight	Delaware, Wilmington	1886
	(Expired-?)	
	Editor & Publisher: A. W. Brinckley	
Delta News	Alabama, Mobile	1894
	(Expired-?)	
	Editor: T. J. Ellis	
The Democrat	North Carolina, Greensboro	
	[Office of Publication:] Box 2430	
Denver Star	Colorado, Denver	
	[Office of Publication:] 910 Twentieth St.	
Detroit Contender	Michigan, Detroit	1920
	(Expired 3-7-21)	
	Issues on File: Detroit Public Library 11-13-20; 3-7-21	
Detroit Informer	Michigan, Detroit	1897
	(Expired 1916)	
	Issue on File: Library of Congress 1-13-00	
Detroit Tribune	Michigan, Detroit	1922
	Editor: J. E. McCall	
	Office of Publication: 2146 St. Antoine St.	
Douglass' Paper, Frederick (1847–1851 as *North Star*)	New York, Rochester	12-3-1847
	(Expired 8-1863)	
	Issues on File: Connecticut State Library, Hartford 10-11-57	
	Yale University, New Haven 2-1-56, 2-17-60	
	Library of Congress (1851) 6-26, 7-24, 7-31, 8-21, 9-4, 9-23, 9-30, 10-9, 10-23, 10-30, 11-13, 12-11, 12-25; (1852) 1-8, 2-13, 3-4,	

3-18, 4-5-20, 6-17, 7-1, 8-
13, 8-20, 10-1, 10-15, 11-
5, 11-19, 12-24; (1853) 8-
19, 9-30, 11-25, 12-9;
(1855) 3-24, 9-8, 8-29,
11-17, 11-21; (1856) 2-1,
2-29, 3-7, 3-21, 6-6, 6-27,
9-26; 6-19-57; (1859) 7-
22, 8-30; 6-8-60
Kansas Hist. Soc., Topeka 2-
2-49; 1852 to 6-1854
Chester County Hist. Soc.,
West Chester, Pennsylva-
nia 6-16-48, 12-1-48
Hampton Institute, Hamp-
ton, Virginia 6-10-52
State Hist. Soc. of Wisconsin, Madison 2-24-54; 2-
23-55; 7-8-59
Public Library of Boston
1847; 2-48 to 1849
Massachusetts Hist. Soc.,
Boston 11-24-48; 12-22-
48
American Antiquarian Soc.,
Worcester, Massachu-
setts (1851) 2-13, 2-27;
(1852) 8-27, 10-29, 11-
12, 2-54, 3-55, 8-55, 10-
12, 11-30-55; (1856) 1-
18, 7-4; (1857) 11-13,
12-4; (1858) 2-12, 5-6, 9-
24, 12-31; 1 to 5-13-59
Johns Hopkins University,
Baltimore, Maryland, 9-
25-51; (1852) 1-15, 2-12,
4-22, 5-7-1, 7-16, 8-13, 8-
27; (1853) 3-18, 4-53, 6-
17, 6-24, 7-15, 9-23, 10-
28, 11-18, 12-16; (1854)
1-6, 6-20, 2-3, 2-17, 3-3,
3-17, 3-31, 5-5, 5-19, 10-
13, 11-10, 12-22; (1855)
1−7-6, 7-20, 10−11-9,
12-14
Public Library, Bangor,
Maine 4-25-56
Michigan University, Ann Arbor (1847 to 1848)
New York State Library, Al-
bany (1859) 7-23, 10-29
Cornell University, Ithaca
1847 to 1-5-49

	New York Hist. Soc. (1848) 8-11, 12-15; (1854) 6-20, 6-27	
	Madison County Hist. Soc., Oneida, New York 1854	
	Syracuse University, Syracuse, New York (1848) 2-11, 2-18; (1854) 12-8, 12-15	
	Oneida Hist. Soc., Utica, New York 3-10-54	
Eagle Dispatch	Louisiana, Baton Rouge [Office of Publication:] 864 S. Thirteenth St.	
East Tennessee News	Tennessee, Knoxville Editor & Publisher: Webster L. Porter, 202 E. Vine Ave. Issues on File: University of Tennessee 12-14-12, 4-29-26, 5-19-32; (1934) 2-1, 11-29, 12-20	1906
Echo	Arkansas, Pine Bluff (Expired-?) Editor: J. C. Duke	1889
Echo	Georgia, Atlanta [Office of Publication:] 917 Gwinnitt St.	
Echo	Georgia, Griffin Editor: A. S. Boynton	1888
Echo	Georgia, Savannah (Expired-?)	1879
Echo	Texas, Beaumont (Expired-?) Editor & Publisher: Wm. M. Smith	1893
Egyptian Sun	Illinois, Mound City [Office of Publication:] 620 Main St.	
Elevator	California, San Francisco (Expired-?) Issues on File: California State Library, Sacramento 10-30-68 Bancroft Library, University of California, Berkeley (1867) 1-15, 8-16; (69 to 70); 12-29-71; (1874) 4-27, 12-27; 12-3-81; 3-2-85; 9-11-86; 10-11-90; 10-8-90; 6-11-98 Kansas Hist. Soc., Topeka 9-8-88	4-6-1865

	American Antiquarian Soc., Worcester, Massachusetts, 3-4-65, 1-11-67; 6-21-67	
	New York State Library, Albany 10-13-65	
Emancipator	Alabama, Montgomery	1917
	(Expired 1920)	
	Issues on File: Dept. of Archives-History, Montgomery 10-17; 8-9-20	
Emancipator and Free American	Massachusetts, Boston (Expired 3-21-1844)	1842
Enterprise	Alabama, Montgomery	1898
	(Expired 1900)	
	Issue on File: Library of Congress 1-26-00	
Enterprise	Georgia, Rome	1903
	(Expired-?)	
	Editor & Publisher: A. T. Atwater	
Enterprise	Illinois, Chicago	1918
Enterprise	Iowa, Sioux City	
	[Office of Publication:] 819 Main St.	
Enterprise	Nebraska, Omaha	1-1893
	(Expired 1914)	
	Issues on File: Library of Congress 1-12-00	
	Nebraska State Hist. Soc., Lincoln (1895) 8-24, 9-21, 10-19, 11-16, 11-30; (1896) 4-18, 5, 6-20, 7, 8-7, 8-19, 8-22, 9-5, 10, 11-14, 12-5, 12-19; (1897) 1-9, 1-23, 2-6, 2-20, 4-3, 4-17, 5-1, 5-15, 5-29, 6-19, 6-26, 7-3; (1908) 8-21, 9-18, 10-2, 10-16, 12; (1909) 6-7-9, 7-30, 8-20, 10-8, 10-29; (1910) 4-22, 5-13, 6-17, 8-15, 8; (1911) 1-6, 1-20, 2	
Enterprise	Virginia, Pulaski	1908
	(Expired 1916)	
	Editor: J. Victor Adams	
Ethiopian World (*Negro World,* 1917–33, *World Peace Echo* 1-6, 4-14-1921; suspended 4-4, 5-26-34)	New York, New York	1917
	Issues on File: Minnesota Hist. Soc., St. Paul 7-3-14-25; 10-17-33; 1-4-14; 5-26-34	
	University of Minnesota 2-17-23; (24 to 26) (29 to 30) (1933)	

	Free Library of Philadelphia 12-20-30; (1932) 1-4 to 14-34	
Evening Recorder (Established in Norfolk as the *Recorder* (weekly) changed to daily except Sunday in 1897. Moved to Newport News 1901; changed to *Evening Recorder,* successor to the *Newport News Star* 11-1901)	Virginia, Newport News (Expired-?)	1893
Fair Play	Kansas, Fort Scott (Expired-?)	1898
Fellowship Herald	Illinois, Chicago	1916
Ferret & Journal of the Lodge	Louisiana, New Orleans (Expired-?) Editor: Dr. E. A. Williams	1891
Flashlight Herald	Tennessee, Knoxville Editor: B. Branner Smith Office of Publication: 1306 College St.	1931
Florida Sentinel	Florida, Jacksonville Issues on File: Library of Congress 1-26-00; 4-19-19	1887
Florida Tattler	Florida, Jacksonville	
Fort Worth Peoples Contender	Texas, Fort Worth [Office of Publication:] 1205 Missouri Avenue	
Forum	Ohio, Dayton Editor & Publisher: John H. Rives	1913
Freedom's Journal* (Also known as *Rights of All*)	New York, New York (Expired 1830) Editors: John Russworm, Samuel Cornish Issues on File: Library of Congress (1828) 3, 5-16, 5-23, 6, 11-21, 12-20 (1829) 1-2, 1-24, 3-28 Public Library of Boston (1828 to 1829) New York State Library, Albany 8-21-27 Cornell University 1827; 3-28 New York Public Library 3-30-27 (facsimile) New York Hist. Soc. (1827) 3-30, 12-21; (1828) 1-18, 3-21, 12-12; (1829) 1-2, 2-14 New Jersey Hist. Soc., Newark, (1827) 4-20, 5-11	3-16-1827

	State Hist. Soc. of Wisconsin, Madison (1827 to 1828)	
	American Antiquarian Soc., Worcester, Massachusetts	
Free Lance	Illinois, Chicago	1895
	(Expired 1926-?)	
	Editor: W. Forrest Cozart	
The Freeman	Indiana, Indianapolis	1884
	(Expired 1926-?)	
	Issues on File: Library of Congress 12-30-99	
	Indiana State Library, Indianapolis 92 to 94; 97-98	
	Indiana Public Library, Indianapolis 7-18-16	
	American Antiquarian Soc., Worcester, Massachusetts 12-2-96	
	New York Public Library (1896) 10-3, 10-10, 10-31; (1897) 2-13, 2-20; 12-24-98; (1902) 1-25, 2-15, 2-22, 3-1, 3-15, 4-5, 5-17, 5-31, 6-21, 7-26, 9-6, 9-27; (1903) 5-9, 5-30, 6-27, 7-18, 7-25, 8-8, 10-3, 10-10, 10-31, 11-14, 11-28, 12-12, 12-26; (1904) 1-9, 2-6, 2-20, 2-27, 3-12, 3-26, 4-2, 4-15, 7-2, 7-16, 8-6, 8-27, 9-10, 9-24, 10-22, 11-4, 12-10, 12-24	
	Ohio State Archeological & Hist. Soc., Columbus 15-20	
Freeman's Chronicle	Connecticut, Hartford	1873
	(Expired-?)	
Free Press	South Carolina, Charleston	1868
	Editor: C. V. Duvall	
	Issues on File: Boston Athenaeum Soc. 4-1 to 5-68	
Free Speech	Illinois, Chicago	1888
	(Expired-?)	
	Editor: J. L. Fleming	
Gary American	Indiana, Gary	1925
	[Office of Publication:] 2085 Broadway	
	Issue on File: Public Library, Gary 11-10-27	
Gasden Call Post	Alabama, Gasden	

Gazette	North Carolina, Raleigh (Expired 1897) Editor & Publisher: James H. Young	1883
Gazette	Ohio, Cleveland [Office of Publication:] 2322 E. Thirtieth St. Issues on File: Library of Congress 1-13-00; 4-6-01 State Library, Boston, Massachusetts 3-15-30 Ohio State Archives & Hist. Soc., Columbus 1-5-01; 3-18	8-25-1883
Georgetown Planet Weekly	South Carolina, Georgetown Editors: James A. Bowley, R. O. Bush Issue on File: Widener Library of Harvard 3-14-74	1873
Georgia Investigator	Georgia, Americus (Expired-?)	1899
Georgia Speaker	Georgia, Atlanta (Expired) [Publisher:] Speaker Publishing Co.	1895
Gleanor	Georgia, Madison (Expired-?) Editor & Publisher: R. G. McAden	1898
Globe	New York, New York (Expired 1884) Issue on File: New York Public Library	1880
Greensboro North Carolina Patriot	North Carolina, Greensboro	
Guardian	Massachusetts, Boston Editor: Wm. Monroe Trotter Issues on File: Massachusetts State Library 1-11-30; 9-31 [Publisher:] Guardian Publishing Company, G. Cornhill	1901
Hartford Advocate	Connecticut, Hartford [Office of Publication:] 14 Mahl Ave.	
Herald	Arkansas, Forrest City (Expired-?) Editor: G. M. Thomason	1896
Herald	Tennessee, Knoxville Editor: Dr. J. H. Presnell [Publisher:] Knoxville Herald Publishing Co., 238 Patton St.	1927

Herald	Texas, Austin	1890
	(Expired 1930-?)	
	Issues on File: Texas University 3-10-17; 6-21-19	
Herald	Virginia, Petersburg	1888
	(Expired-?)	
	Editor & Publisher: Scott Wood	
Herald-Commonwealth	Maryland, Baltimore	1920
	(Expired 193_?)	
	Editor: W. T. Andrews	
Hot Springs Echo	Arkansas, Hot Springs	
	Office of Publication: 405 Malvern Ave.	
Houston Defender	Texas, Houston	10-11-1930
	Issues on File: Public Library, Houston, 1930	
Houston Freeman	Texas, Houston	1893
	(Expired-?)	
	[Publisher:] Freeman Publishing Co., Houston	
Houston Informer (1-10-31 to 7-18-34 as *Houston Informer & Texas Freeman*)	Texas, Houston	5-24-1919
	Office of Publication: 2418 Leeland Ave.	
	Issues on File: Public Library, Houston (1919 to 6-14-24); 8-30	
Houston Observer	Texas, Houston	1916
	(Expired 6-18-21)	
	Issues on File: Public Library, Houston 1-27-17 to 21	
Houston Sentinel	Texas, Houston	1927
	(Expired 10-31-31)	
	Issues on File: Public Library, Houston 27 to 30	
Huntsville Gazette	Alabama, Huntsville	11-22-1872
	(Expired 12-29-94)	
	Editor: Philip Joseph	
	Issues on File: Dept. of Archives & Hist., Montgomery (1881) 3-28, 6-11, 6-18, 7-30, 8-13, 11-12, 12-3	
	Madison County Court House, Huntsville 79 to 86; 3-12-89; 91 to 94	
	Library of Congress 6-18-81 to 12-24-88; 89 to 94	
Huntsville Gazette	Alabama, Huntsville	1879
	(Expired-?)	
	Editor: Charles Hendley, Jr.	
	Publishers: Huntsville Gazette Co.	

Huntsville Herald	Alabama, Huntsville (Expired 1883) Editor: W. H. Council	1878
Huntsville News	Alabama, Huntsville (Expired 1923) Issues on File: Dept. of Ar- chives & Hist., Montgom- ery 1-23; 2-19-23 Madison County Court House, Huntsville 10-30- 13-22	1917
Huntsville Star	Alabama, Huntsville Issue on File: Library of Con- gress 1-26-00	1-26-1900
Hutchinson Blade	Kansas, Hutchinson (Expired 1922) Issues on File: Kansas Hist. Soc., Topeka 12-20-19; 4-1- 22	1914
Illinois Conservator	Illinois, Springfield Editor: F. L. Rogers, 725½ E. Washington St.	1905
Illinois Crusader	Illinois, East Saint Louis Office of Publication: 3 N. Fif- teenth St.	
Illinois Times	Illinois, Champaign Editor & Publisher: Edgar G. Harris, 208 Ells Ave.	1939
Independent	Georgia, Atlanta (Expired 1933) Editor: B.J. Davis [Publisher:] Independent Pub- lishing Corp.	1903
Independent	Kentucky, Ashland	
Independent	Michigan, Detroit (Expired-?) Editor: Wm. J. Robinson [Publisher:] Detroit Indepen- dent Publishing Co., 2906 St. Antoine St.	1922
Index*	Tennessee, Memphis (Expired-?) [Publisher:] The Index Publish- ing Co., 3395 Second St.	1923
Indianapolis Recorder	Indiana, Indianapolis Editor & Publisher: Marcus Stewart Office of Publication: 518 Indi- ana Ave. Issues on File: Indiana State Li- brary, Indianapolis 1899; 12-06; 3-32 Indianapolis Public Library, Indianapolis 1899; 1916	1897

Indianapolis World	Indiana, Indianapolis	1883
	(Expired 1920)	
	Issue on File: Library of Congress 1-27-00	
Indicator	Kentucky, Hopkinsville	1893
	(Expired-?)	
	Editor: Peter Boyd	
Industrial Day	Virginia, Richmond	1888
	(Expired 1890-?)	
	Editor: Joseph T. Wilson	
Industrial Era	Texas, Beaumont	1903
	Editor & Publisher:	
	O. Kirkwood	
Informer	Kentucky, Louisville	1887
	(Expired-?)	
	Editor: H. H. Hatcher	
	Publisher: 517 W. Walnut St.	
Interpreter	Virginia, Lynchburg	1903
	(Expired 1906)	
	Editor: Robert W. Goff	
Iowa Observer	Iowa, Des Moines	
	Office of Publication: 515 Mulberry St.	
Item	Texas, Dallas	18__
	(Expired-?)	
	Editor: Ellis Willis	
	Publishers: I. G. Griffin & E. Willis	
Item	Texas, Fort Worth	1890
	(Expired-?)	
	[Publisher:] Item Publishing Co.	
Jamaica Gleaner	Long Island, Jamaica	
	[Office of Publication:] 166-11 Hendrickson Place	
Journal (1895–96 as *Huntsville Journal*)	Alabama, Huntsville	1895
	(Expired 1912)	
	Issues on File: Dept. of Archives & Hist., Montgomery 8-99 to 2-12	
	Madison County Court House, Huntsville 1895; 1903; 08; 10; 11	
Journal	Alabama, Huntsville	1895
	(Expired-?)	
	Editor: H. C. Binford	
Journal	Georgia, Savannah	1918
	(Expired-?)	
	[Publisher:] Savannah Journal Publishing Co., 725 W. Broad St.	

Journal	Pennsylvania, Pittsburgh	1893
	(Expired-?)	
	Editor: S. I. R. Hoodes	
Journal and Guide	Virginia, Norfolk	1901
	Publisher: P. B. Young, Sr.	
	Office of Publication: 711-24 E. Olney Road	
	Issues on File: Fisk University 33-34	
	YMCA Graduate School, Nashville, Tennessee 1928 to 10-15-32	
	Hampton Institute 1935	
	Virginia State College for Negroes, Petersburg, 9-31	
*Kansas City Advocate**	Kansas, Kansas City	1914
	(Expired 1926)	
	Issues on File: Kansas Hist. Soc., Topeka 5-26-15; 3-7-26	
Kansas City American	Missouri, Kansas City	4-12-1928
	Issues on File: Missouri Hist. Soc. 6-21-28 to 1-12-33	
Kansas City Observer	Missouri, Kansas City	1896
	(Expired 1901)	
	Issue on File: Library of Congress 1-27-00	
Kansas City Sun	Missouri, Kansas City	1908
	(Expired 1924)	
	Issues on File: Kansas Hist. Soc., Topeka 12-7-12	
	Missouri Hist. Soc., Columbia 1-10-14; 6-24	
Kansas Elevator	Kansas, Kansas City	1916
	(Expired 1918)	
	Issues on File: Kansas Hist. Soc., Topeka 2-12-16, 11-4-16	
Kansas Herald and Freedom	Kansas, Lawrence	1855
	(Expired-?)	
	Issues on File: Yale University Library (1855) 7-8, 11-10, 11-29, 12-1, 12-15; (1856) 1-12, 5-3, 11-1, 12-27; (1857) 1-3, 2-7, 2-21, 2-27, 3-14, 4-11, 6-27	
Kansas State Ledger	Kansas, Topeka	1892
	(Expired-?)	
	Editor: F. L. Jeltz	
Kansas Watchman	Kansas, Topeka	1903
	(Expired 1905)	
	Issues on File: Kansas Hist. Soc., Topeka 3-25, 11-15-05	

Kentucky Reporter	Kentucky, Louisville (Expired-?) Editor: R. T. Berry Office of Publication: 930 Walnut St.	1899
Knoxville Negro World (Daily)	Tennessee, Knoxville Publishers: Patterson Bros. & Co.	1887
Laboring Man (Established as *The Laborer.* Edited by J. A. Penn; changed to *Laboring Man* 1887 and edited by P. H. Johnson)	Virginia, Lynchburg (Expired 1887-?)	1886
Lake County Observer	Indiana, Gary Editor: Charles P. Howard, Jr. Publisher: Howard Newspaper Syndicate, Inc., 1629 Massachusetts St.	1946
Leader (Established 1888 or 1890, M. L. Robinson, editor, merged with the *Clipper* (Leader & Clipper Publishing Co.) 1894–1898. Title of *Leader* resumed)	Virginia, Alexandria (Expired 1900)	1888
Leavenworth Advocate	Kansas Leavenworth (Expired 1891) Issues on File: Kansas Hist. Soc., Topeka 8-18-88, 8-22-91	1888
Lexington Standard	Kentucky, Lexington (Expired 1912) Issues on File: Library of Congress 1-27-00 Transylvania College, Lexington 3-00; 2-7-03	1892
Liberator	Missouri, Kansas City Issue on File: Missouri Hist. Soc., Columbia, 1903	2-1901
Light	Mississippi, Vicksburg (Expired 1895) Editor: W. H. Rogers	1891
Lighthouse and Informer	South Carolina, Columbia Editor & Publisher: John H. McCray	1937
The Listener	New York, Bronx [Office of Publication:] 797 E. 166th St.	
Los Angeles Sentinel	California, Los Angeles Editor: Loren Miller	1932

	Publisher: Leon H. Washington, Jr., 1050 E. Forty-third Place	
Los Angeles Tribune	California, Los Angeles Editor: Almena Davis Publisher: Lucius W. Lomax, Jr., 4225 S. Central Ave.	1940
Louisiana Republican	Louisiana, New Orleans (Expired-?)	1881
The Louisianian Daily (The *New Orleans Semi-Weekly Louisianian* — or *The New Orleans Weekly Louisianian*)	Louisiana, New Orleans (Expired 6-17-88) Editors: John Sella, P. S. B. Pinchback Issues on File: Library of Congress 12-18-70 to 1-25-73; 8-15-75; 3-27-75, 11-30-78, 6-17-82 Texas University Austin 5-14-71; 2-28-74; 2-5-76; 9-29-77; 6-17-82	12-18-1870
Louisville Defender	Kentucky, Louisville Editor: Frank L. Stanley Office of Publication: 418 S. Fifth St.	1933
Louisville Leader	Kentucky, Louisville Editor & Publisher: O. Willis Cole Office of Publication: 930 W. Walnut St.	1917
Loyal Georgian	Georgia, Augusta Issues on File: University of Georgia 8-10-67; 8-24-67 Boston Athenaeum, Boston (1866) 1-20, 2-3, 2-17, 3-3, 3-17, 5-5; (1867) 4-10, 5-9, 5-16, 7-6 American Antiquarian Soc., Worcester, Massachusetts 10-13-66 Duke University, Durham, North Carolina 2-24-66; 2-15-68	1866
Macon Sentinel	Georgia, Macon (Expired 1900-?) Issues on File: Library of Congress 1-27-00	1899
Major	Kentucky, Hopkinsville (Expired-?) Editor & Publisher: A. C. Banks	1897

McDowell Times	West Virginia, Keystone	1913
	(Expired-?)	
	[Office of Publication:] Box 447	
	Issues on File: West Virginia	
	State Library 5-13 +	
Memphis Journal	Tennessee, Memphis	
	[Office of Publication:] 390½	
	Beale St.	
Memphis World	Tennessee, Memphis	1931
(Semi-weekly)	Editor: L. O. Swingler	
	Publisher: Scott Newspaper	
	Syndicate, 388 Beale Ave.	
Messenger*	South Carolina, Charleston	1894
	(Expired-?)	
	Publishers: Orphan Aid Society,	
	20 Franklin St.	
Messenger*	Texas, Waco	1932
	Editor & Publisher: L. J.	
	Rhone, 109 Bridge St.	
Messenger*	West Virginia, Charleston	
	Office of Publication: 1315	
	Washington St.	
Metropolitan Journal	Alabama, Birmingham	1892
	(Expired-?)	
	Editor: Rev. Wm. McGill	
Miami Times	Florida, Miami	1923
	Editor & Publisher: H. E. S.	
	Reeves	
	Office of Publication: 1112	
	N.W. Third Ave.	
Miami Whip	Florida, Miami	1943
	Editor & Publisher: Sam B. Sol-	
	oman, 221 N.W. Ninth St.	
Michigan Chronicle	Michigan, Detroit	1936
	Editor: L. E. Martin	
	Office of Publication: 268 E.	
	Eliot St.	
Michigan Independent	Michigan, (?)	1922
(1922 to 3-24-35 as *Indepen-*		
dent; 1935 as *Northwestern*		
News)		
Michigan State News	Michigan, Grand Rapids	1920
	(Expired 1925)	
	Issues on File: Public Library,	
	Grand Rapids 2-9-22; 1-3-	
	25	
Midwest Post	Indiana, Indianapolis	
Mind	Texas, Fort Worth	1931
	Office of Publication: 915½	
	Calhoun St.	

Minneapolis Spokesman	Minnesota, Minneapolis	1934
	Editor & Publisher: C. E. New-man	
	Office of Publication: 314 Third St., South	
*Mirror**	Missouri, St. Joseph	1886
	(Expired-?)	
Missionary Record	South Carolina, Charleston	1871
	Editor: R. H. Cain	
	Issue on File: Widener Library of Harvard 8-26-71	
Mobile Weekly Press-Forum	Alabama, Mobile	1894
	(Expired 1928)	
	Issues on File: Dept. of Archives & Hist., Montgomery (1914) 1-10, 2-21, 8-1; 11-21 to 28; 4-29; 6-30, 33 to 9-34	
*Monitor**	Louisiana, Donaldsonville	
Monitor	Louisiana, New Orleans	1893
	(Expired-?)	
	Editor: C. F. Meine	
	Publishers: Monitor Publishing Co., 60 Corondolet St.	
Muskogee Lantern	Oklahoma, Muskogee	1902
(Expired 1926 as *Watchman*	(Expired 1926)	
& *Lantern*)	Editor: Napoleon Scott, Jr.	
Muskogee Republican	Oklahoma, Muskogee	1905
	(Expired 1912-?)	
	Issue on File: Oklahoma Hist. Soc., Oklahoma City 1912	
Muskogee Star	Oklahoma, Muskogee	1912
	Issues on File: Oklahoma Hist. Soc., Oklahoma City 1912	
*Nashville Globe**	Tennessee, Nashville	1906
(*Globe Independent*)	Issues on File: Fisk University 1935	
National Era	District of Columbia, Washington	1847
	(Expired-?)	
	Issues on File: Duke University, Durham (1847) 9-30, 10 & 12; (1849) 55 complete 57-58	
	Library of Congress (complete)	
	Public Library, Boston (complete)	
National Independent	Michigan, Detroit	1891
	(Expired-?)	
	Publisher: George R. Nevels, 149-151 Randolph St.	

National Negro Voice	Louisiana, New Orleans	12-16-1913
	(Expired 1916)	
	Editor & Publisher: R. A. Flynn	
National Reflector	Kansas, Wichita	1895
	(Expired 1897-?)	
	Issues on File: Kansas Hist. Soc., Topeka 12-8-95 to 97	
National Republican	Georgia, Greenville	1898
	(Expired-?)	
	Editor: Rev. J. H. Grant	
Negro Appeal	Maryland, Annapolis	1899
	(Expired 1900)	
	Issue on File: Library of Congress 2-16-00	
Negro Criterion	Virginia, Richmond	1905
	(Expired 1909)	
	Editors: Giles B. Jackson & W. S. Blackburn	
Negro Gazette	Louisiana, New Orleans	9-18-1872
	Editor: R. I. Cromwell	
	Issue on File: Boston Athenaeum Soc.	
Negro Journal of Industry	Tennessee, Memphis	
	Office of Publication: 714 Mississippi Ave.	
Negro Labor News	Texas, Houston	1931
	Editor & Publisher: C. W. Rice	
	Office of Publication: 419½ Milam St.	
Negro Star	Kansas, Wichita	1908
	(Expired-?)	
	Issues on File: Kansas Hist. Soc., Topeka 3-20	
Negro Watchman	Alabama, Montgomery	1874
	(Expired-?)	
	Assistant Editor: William H. Council	
Negro World (Daily & weekly)	New York, New York	1919
	(Expired 1933)	
Negro World	Tennessee, Knoxville	11-17-1887
	(Expired 1895)	
	Issues on File: Library of Congress (1888) 8-10, 11-24; 2-2-81; 3-7-92	
	University of Illinois, Urbana 2-3-88	
	Lawson McGhee Library, Knoxville, Tennessee (1887) 10-15; 11-26	
New Age-Dispatch	California, Los Angeles	1904
	(Expired-?)	
	Publisher: New Age Publishing Co., 4200 S. Central Ave.	

New Era	Delaware, Wilmington	1899
	(Expired-?)	
	Editor: C. Marcellus Dorsey	
	Publisher: New Era Publishing	
	Co., 511 Market St.	
New Idea	Alabama, Selma	1891
	(Expired-?)	
	Editor: J. M. Gee	
New Jersey Herald Guardian	New Jersey, Newark	
	[Office of Publication:] 129 W. Market St.	
New Jersey Herald News	New Jersey, Newark	1927
	Editor: Dr. Marc Mooreland	
	Office of Publication: 130 E. Kenney St.	
New Jersey Record	New Jersey, Newark	1934
	Editor: F. R. Clark	
	Publisher: New Jersey Record Publishing Co., 129 W. Market St.	
New Jersey Trumpet	New Jersey, Newark	1887
	(Expired-?)	
	Editor: Wm. Murrell	
New Light	Arkansas, Forrest City	1899
	(Expired-?)	
	Editor: Rev. Emanuel Johnson	
New National Era	District of Columbia, Washington	1869
	(Expired after 1874)	
	Editors: Lewis H. Douglass, J. Seall Martin	
	Issues on File: W. 135th Street Public Library, New York 3-1 to 6-73	
New Orleans Daily Creole	Louisiana, New Orleans	1857
	(Expired-?)	
New Orleans Sentinel	Louisiana, New Orleans	
	Office of Publication: 2407 Third St.	
Newport News Post	Virginia, Newport News	
	Office of Publication: 511 Twenty-fifth St.	
Newport News Star	Virginia, Newport News	1901
(Established by Matthew N. Lewis as successor to his *Evening Recorder* edited by Lewis, 1901–1926 when he died; by J. Thomas Newsome 1926)	Issues on File: Hampton Institute (1921) 2-24; (1931) 9-3; (1932) 3-17, 4-7; (1933) 3-30, 6-15, 10-26, 12-7; (1935) 8-17, 8-31	

New South	Kentucky, Louisville	1894
	(Expired-?)	
	Editor: Albert S. White	
	Office of Publication: New South Publishing Co., 517 W. Walnut St.	
New York Age (1880-11-8-1884 as *New York Globe;* 11-22-12-6-1884 *Freeman;* 12-13-1884, 10-8-1883 *New York Freeman*)	New York, New York Office of Publication: 230 W. 135th St. Publisher: Fred R. Moore Corp. Issues on File: Yale University, New Haven 5-2-85 Library of Congress 11-18-82-83, 11-18-92; 1-4-00 Public Library of Boston 4-87, (1888) 7-9, 7-16, 9-1, 2-7-89; 8-16-90; 2-92 New York State Library, Albany 3-7-85 New York Public Library 1906 to 1909; 1911 New York Hist. Soc., 2-13-92 YMCA Graduate School, Nashville 2-31 to 9-2-33	1880
New York News	New York, New York (Expired 193_?) Publisher: Job Printing Corp.	1913
North Jersey News	New Jersey, Montclair Office of Publication: 20 Elwood Ave.	
Northwest Enterprise	Washington, Seattle [Office of Publication:] P.O. Box 1873	1920
Northwestern Recorder * (4-1892 to 11-26-1892 as *Wisconsin Afro-American*)	Wisconsin, Milwaukee (Expired 3-1893) Issues on File: State Hist. Soc. of Wisconsin, Madison	4-1892
Northwest Herald	Washington, Seattle Editor & Publisher: S. T. McCants, 2203 E. Madison St.	1935
Oakland Independent (*Western American*)	California, Oakland Issues on File: Bancroft Library, University of California, Berkeley 7-8-71 to 2-74	
Oakland Times	California, Oakland (Expired-?) Issues on File: Bancroft Library & University of California, Berkeley 8-29-23	9-29-1923

Observer	Louisiana, Baton Rouge (Expired 1900) Issue on File: Howard Memorial Library, New Orleans 1-13-00	1899
Observer	Missouri, Kansas City Publisher: L. C. Williams	1896
Ohio Express	Ohio, Springfield	
Ohio Falls Express	Kentucky, Louisville (Expired 1904) Issues on File: University of Chicago, Chicago, Illinois 7-11-91	1878
Ohio Republican	Ohio, Cincinnati (Expired-?)	1884
Ohio State News	Ohio, Columbus Office of Publication: 867 Mt. Vernon St.	1942
Ohio State Tribune	Ohio, Springfield (Expired-?)	1884
Oklahoma Eagle	Oklahoma, Tulsa Editor: Theo. Boughman Publisher: Mrs. R. C. Boughman	1922
Oklahoma Independent	Oklahoma, Muskogee Office of Publication: 115½ S. Second St.	
Omaha Guide	Nebraska, Omaha Issues on File: Nebraska Hist. Soc. (1932) 7-16; 7-23; 8-6; 9	1927
Omaha Monitor	Nebraska, Omaha (Expired 1-11-29) Editor: John Albert Williams Issues on File: Nebraska Hist. Soc. (1915) 7-6; 9-4; 9-18; 9-27	7-3-1915
Palladium	Missouri, St. Louis (Expired-?) Editor: J. W. Wheeler Publisher: W. E. Henderson, 2016 Chestnut St.	1899
Palmetto Leader	South Carolina, Columbia Editor: N. J. Frederick Publisher: G. H. Hampton, 1310 Assembly St.	1925

People's Advocate	District of Columbia, Washington (Expired 1886) Editor: J. W. Cromwell Issues on File: Rather complete file in possession of daughter, Dr. Otelia Cromwell, Washington, District of Columbia	1876
People's Advocate	Georgia, Atlanta (Expired-?) Publisher: People's Paper Publishing Co., 40 N. Forseyth St.	1891
People's Choice	Alabama, Opelika (Expired-?) Editor: P. Lawrence Publisher: East Alabama Publishing Co.	1894
People's Defender	Mississippi, Jackson (Expired 1895) Editor: W. Newman Publisher: People's Publishing Co.	1889
People's Elevator	Kansas, Independence (Expired 1931) Issues on File: Kansas Hist. Soc., Topeka 2-31-24; 4-30	1924
People's Elevator	Kansas, Kansas City [Office of Publication:] 503 N. Sixth St.	1892
People's Light	Virginia, Pulaski (Expired-?) Editor: R. J. Buckner	1893
The People's Voice	New York, New York Office of Publication: 210 West 125th St.	1942
Petersburg Herald	Virginia, Petersburg (Expired 1899) Issue on File: Virginia Hist. Soc., Richmond 12-31-92	188_
Philadelphia Independent	Pennsylvania, Philadelphia Office of Publication: 1708 Lombard St.	1931
Philadelphia Tribune	Pennsylvania, Philadelphia Editor: Eustace Gay Office of Publication: 526 S. Sixteenth St. Issues on File: Free Library of Philadelphia 11-28-25; 6-27	1884

Pittsburgh Courier	Pennsylvania, Pittsburgh Office of Publication: 2628 Centre Ave. Issues on File: Pennsylvania State Library, Harrisburg 3-25-11 and 12-33; 1934 Library of Congress	1907
Pittsburgh Examiner	Pennsylvania, Pittsburgh Office of Publication: 2132 Centre Ave.	
Plain-Dealer	Georgia, Valdosta (Expired-?) Editor: E. H. Quo	1898
Plaindealer	Kansas, Topeka Editor: Nick Chiles (Now published in Kansas City) Office of Publication: 1612 N. Fifth St.	1899
Post	North Carolina, Charlotte Editor & Publisher: H. Houston	1926
Press	Alabama, Mobile (Expired-?) Publisher: Press Publishing Co.	1894
Press	Virginia, Port Royal (Expired 1898) Editor: George R. Pratt	1893
Press (Established 1891 by the *Roa-noke Daily Press* as an afternoon paper; became a weekly in 1894 — John H. Davis, editor)	Virginia, Roanoke (Expired 1897)	1891
Progress	Arkansas, Helena (Expired-?) Editor: T. B. Littlejohn	1880
Progress	Nebraska, Omaha (Expired 1904) Issues on File: Library of Con-gress 1-26-00 Nebraska State Hist. Soc., Lincoln, (1890) 3-22, 11-29; 3-7-91	1889
Progressive Age	Louisiana, Alexandria (Expired-?) Editor & Publisher: A. J. Touis-sant & Co.	1897
Progressive Herald	New York, Syracuse Editor & Publisher: J. Luther Sylvahn, 815 E. Fayette St.	1933
Public Ledger (Daily)	Indiana, Baltimore Editor: John Wesley Adams	1887

Race Standard	Maryland, Baltimore (Expired 1898) Issues on File: Enoch Pratt Free Library (1897) 1-2; 1-16	1894
Radical	Missouri, St. Joseph (Expired-?) Editor: Isaac Frederick Publisher: Radical Publishing Co.	1897
Ram's Horn	New York, New York (Expired June 1848) Editors: Willis A. Hodges and Thomas Van Rensselaer	1847
Record	Louisiana, Shreveport (Expired-?) Editor: E. D. Minton	1896
Record	North Carolina, Asheville [Office of Publication:] P.O. Box 1149	
Recorder	Virginia, Norfolk (Expired-?) Editor: M. N. Lewis	1893
The Reformer	Virginia, Richmond (Expired 1931) Issues on File: Library of Con- gress 1-27-00 Texas University, Austin 5-24- 13	1895
Register	Missouri, Hannibal (Expired-?) Editor: G. H. Wright	1919
Register	Texas, San Antonio Editor: J. T. Duncan Publisher: V. C. Bellinger Office of Publication: 207 N. Centre St.	1931
Reporter	Alabama, Birmingham Editor: O. W. Adams, 1163 Fourth Ave., North	1902
Reporter	Georgia, Atlanta (Expired-?) Editor: A. A. Gordon	1895
Reporter	Mississippi, Natchez Publisher: Reporter Publishing Co.	1909
Reporter	Virginia, Richmond (Expired 1893) Editor: John Clinton	1890
Republican	New York, New York (Expired-?) Editor: W. R. Davis, 153 W. Twenty-seventh St.	1896

Rescue	Louisiana, New Orleans	1893
	(Expired-?)	
	Editor & Publisher: Simms & Gould	
Review	Virginia, Petersburg	
	(Expired 1925)	
	Editor: A. B. Mackey	
Richmond Planet	Virginia, Richmond	1883
	Issues on File: Library of Congress 1900	
	Widener Library of Harvard 90-13; 25-30	
	American Antiquarian Soc., Worcester, Massachusetts 1886 (1889) 6-12, 6-8; 6-95; (1901) 5-12, 7-12; (1917) 31; 35 (1889) 6-8, (95 to 01: 6-29) (1917) 5-12, (January to December) (1918) 31-3: 1935	
	Hampton Institute 1935	
	State Hist. Soc. of Wisconsin 6-26-19	
	University of Virginia 11-26-32, 6-16-34; (1935) 6-30, 9-22, 10-13, 11-10, 11-24; 6-26-19	
Right House	Kentucky, (?)	1908
	(Expired-?)	
	Editor: Thomas A. Lawrence	
Rights of All (Formerly *Freedom's Journal;* See)	New York, New York	
Rising Sun	Iowa, Des Moines	1883
	(Expired-?)	
Rising Sun	Missouri, Kansas City	1896
	(Expired 1918)	
	Issues on File: Library of Congress 1-27-00	
	Missouri Hist. Soc. 1-16-03 to 07	
Rochester Voice	New York, Rochester	1933
	Publisher: H. W. Coles, 446 Clarissa St.	
St. Louis American	Missouri, St. Louis	1928
	Editor & Publisher: N. A. Sweets, 11 N. Jefferson St.	
	Issues on File: St. Louis Public Library 1928 to date	

St. Louis Argus	Missouri, St. Louis	1912
	Editor: J. E. Mitchell	
	Publisher: St. Louis Argus Publishing Co., 2312 Market St.	
	Issues on File: Missouri Hist. Soc. 15 to 18; 2-19	
	St. Louis Public Library 8-32 to date	
	YMCA Graduate School, Nashville, Tennessee 10-11-18; 11-29; (1930) 3, 8-15, 9-26, 10; (1931) 9-11, 10-23, 11-13, 11-27, 12-11; (1932) 1, 2-19, 3-19; 4-15, 4-22, 5-20, 6-24, 7-15, 8-5, 10-14, 11-11, 12; 11-33; 3-34	
St. Louis Clarion	Missouri, St. Louis (Expired 1922)	1915
St. Louis Recorder	Missouri, St. Louis	1943
St. Paul Recorder	Minnesota, St. Paul	1934
	Editor & Publisher: C. E. Newman, 357 Minnesota St.	
San Antonio Inquirer	Texas, San Antonio	
	[Office of Publication:] Box 98	
San Antonio Register	Texas, San Antonio	1931
	Editor: U. J. Andrews	
	Publisher: V. C. Bellinger, 207 N. Centre St.	
San Francisco Reporter	California, San Francisco	194_
	Editor: Thomas C. Fleming	
San Francisco Sentinel	California, San Francisco (Expired-?)	18__
	[Office of Publication:] 502 Montgomery St.	
	Editor: R. C. O. Benjamin	
Savannah Tribune	Georgia, Savannah	1875
	Editor & Publisher: Sol. C. Johnson	
Savannah Weekly Echo	Georgia, Savannah (Expired-?)	1879
	Issues on File: New York Hist. Soc. (1883) 8-26, 12-2; (1884) 1-13, 1-20, 2-3, 2-10	
Searchlight	Louisiana, Lake Charles (Expired-?)	1898
	Editor & Publisher: J. S. Jones	
Seattle Republican	Washington, Seattle (Expired 1915)	1894
	Issues on File: Library of Congress 1-19-00	
	Washington State Library 1908, 4-1913	

Sedalia Times	Missouri, Sedalia	1894
	(Expired 1905)	
	Issues on File: Missouri Hist.	
	Soc. 8-31-01, 12-19-03;	
	(1905) 1-21, 2-4	
Sentinel	District of Columbia, Wash-	1850
	ington	
	Editor: West A. Hamilton	
Sentinel	Georgia, Augusta	1885
	(Expired-?)	
	Editor: Silas Xavier Floyd	
Sepia Socialite	Louisiana, New Orleans	1936
(Changed to *The Negro*	[Office of Publication:] 1241–	
South, monthly magazine,	43 Dryades St.	
January, 1946)		
Shreveport Sun	Louisiana, Shreveport	10-6-1920
	Editor: M. L. Collins	
Signal	Maryland, Cumberland	1897
	Editor: W. H. Thomas	
South Carolina Leader	South Carolina, Charleston	1865
	(Expired about 1868)	
	Editors: A. Coffin, H. Judge	
	Moore, Timothy Hurley &	
	Richard H. Cain	
	Issues on File: Boston Athenae-	
	um Society (1865) 10-7-21;	
	12-9-23; (1866) 3-31; 5-12	
Southern Age	Georgia, Atlanta	1891
	Editor: H. A. Hagler	
Southern American	Tennessee, Chattanooga	1884
	Editor: H. C. Smith	
Southern News	Georgia, Savannah	18__
	Editor: Rev. T. N. M. Smith	
Southern News	North Carolina, Asheville	
	[Office of Publication:] P.O.	
	Box 464	
Southern News	Virginia, Richmond	1890
	(Expired 1894)	
	Issue on File: Henry E. Hunt-	
	ington LB, San Marino,	
	California, 10-15-92	
Southern Sentinel	Alabama, [?]	1896
	(Expired 1899)	
	Editor: R. I. Ruffin	
Southwestern Christian	Pennsylvania, Philadelphia	18__
Advocate	(Expired-?)	
	Editor: L. J. Coppin	
Standard	Kentucky, Lexington	1892
	(Expired-?)	
Standard	Virginia, Norfolk	1889
	(Expired 1891)	
	Editors: Landon Jessup, D.	
	Betts Robinson	

Standard Echo	Pennsylvania, Philadelphia	1881
	Editor: P. Caldwell	
Star	Virginia, Newport News	1903
	[Publisher:] Star Publishing Co.	
State Capital	Illinois, Springfield	1886
	Editor: Jordon S. Murray	
Statesman	Colorado, Denver	1889
	Editor: Edward H. Hackley	
Sunday Item	District of Columbia, Wash-ington	1881
	(Expired-?)	
Sunday Unionist	Kentucky, Owensboro	1894
	(Expired-?)	
	Editor: J. M. Griffin	
Sunset Community Leader	Indiana, Indianapolis	
	[Office of Publication:] 322 N. Senate Ave.	
Tampa Bulletin	Florida, Tampa	1915
	Editor: M. D. Potter, P.O. Box 2232	
Tennessee Star	Tennessee, (?)	1886
	(Expired 1891)	
	Issue on File: Lawson-McGhee Library, Knoxville 11-25-87	
Texas Examiner	Texas, Houston	1942
	Editor & Publisher: Rev. L. V. Bolton, 4520½ Lyons Ave.	
Texas Headlight	Texas, Austin	1895
	(Expired-?)	
	Editor: D. A. Scott	
Times	Missouri, Sedalia	1894
	(Expired 1905-?)	
	Editor: W. H. Carter	
	Issues on File: Missouri Hist. Soc. 8-31-01; 12-19-03; (1905) 1-21, 2-4	
Times Observer	Kansas, (?)	1888
	(Expired 1892)	
	Issues on File: Kansas Hist. Soc., Topeka 9-91; 9-10-92	
Topeka Call	Kansas, Topeka	1880
	(Expired 1898)	
	Issues on File: Kansas Hist. Soc. 6-28-91; 10-98	
Topeka Tribune	Kansas, Topeka	1880
	(Expired 1881)	
	Issues on File: Kansas Hist. Soc. 6-24-80; 10-81	
Tribune	Georgia, Savannah	1886
	[Publisher:] Tribune Publishing Co.	
Tribune	Kansas, Wichita	1898
	Editor: D. L. Robinson	

Tribune	Virginia, Staunton (Expired 1933) Editor: W. C. Brown	19__

*La Tribune de La
  Nouvelle-Orleans**
(Daily)
	Louisiana, New Orleans
	(Expired 1870)
	Editor: C. J. Dalloz
	Issues on File: Howard Library
	  of New Orleans 1864, 1865,
	  1866, 1867
	Archives of City of New Or-
	  leans 7-21-64; 12-67
	Boston Athenaeum Society
	  1864 through 1870
		1864

Tri-County Bulletin	California, San Bernardino Editor: J. Robert Smith, 622 Harris St.	1945
True Reformer	North Carolina, Littleton Issue on File: Duke University, Durham 7-25-00	1899
Tuskegee Messenger	Alabama, Tuskegee Institute	
Twin City Observer	Minnesota, Minneapolis Editor: Milton G. Williams, 305 S. Fifth St.	1943

Union	Ohio, Cincinnati
	Editor: W. P. Dabney
	Office of Publication: 412
	  McAllister St.
	Issues on File: Ohio Hist. Soc.,
	  Columbus 1916–19; 1913–
	  23
		1907

Union (L'Union)
  (In French & English)
	Louisiana, New Orleans
	Issues on File: Archives of the
	  City of New Orleans (1863)
	  1-13, 1-15, 1-29, 2-24, 2-28,
	  4-9, 4-16, 5-14, 5-19, 5-30,
	  6-2, 6-30, 8-1, 12-25
	Boston Athenaeum Society 2-
	  11-64
	Western Reserve Hist. Soc. 7-
	  9-63; (1864) 7-12, 7-19
	Wisconsin Hist. Soc. (62-64)
		1862

Valley Index	Virginia, Staunton (Expired 1905) Editors: James M. Morris, Mil- lon S. Malone	1897

Vindicator	California, San Francisco
	(Expired 1906)
	Editor: J. E. Brown
	Issues on File: Bancroft Library
	  University of California,
	  Berkeley (1887) 5-2, 5-16,
	  6-11, 6-25, 7, 8-30
	Kansas Hist. Soc., Topeka 11-
	  17-88, 2-9-89; 2-16-89
		1884

Vindicator	Louisiana, New Orleans	18__
	Editor: T. B. Stamps	
Virginia Star	Virginia, Richmond	4-1877
	(Expired 1888)	
	Issues on File: Virginia Hist.	
	Soc. 9-8-77	
	Virginia State Library, Rich-	
	mond (1878) 5-11, 12-14;	
	3-27-80; (1881) 4-30, 8-	
	27; (1882) 11-11; 11-18,	
	12-9, 12-23	
Voice	Virginia, Richmond	1918
	(Expired 1925)	
	Editors: Benjamin F. Vaughan,	
	Wallace Van Jackson	
Voice Newspaper*	New York, Rochester	
	[Office of Publication:] 397½	
	Clarissa St.	
Voice of Colorado	Colorado, Colorado Springs	
Voice of Ethiopia	New York, New York	
	[Office of Publication:] 2352	
	Seventh Ave.	
Voice of the People	Alabama, (?)	1913
	(Expired 1924)	
	Issues on File: Dept. of Ar-	
	chives & Hist., Montgom-	
	ery 6-1916-19; 1-7-22; 1-9-	
	22	
Washington American	District of Columbia, Wash-	1-1909
	ington	
	Issues on File: Library of Con-	
	gress (1911) 3-11, 5-27, 8-	
	12, 8-19; 9	
Washington Bee	District of Columbia, Wash-	1-3-1882
(1882 to 7-1884 as *Bee.* Sus-	ington	
pended from 1-14 to 1-28-	(Expired 1-21-1922)	
93; from Feb. to Apr. 1895)	Issues on File: Library of Con-	
	gress (1882) 6-10, 6-24, 12-	
	25; (93-96) (1905)-22	
	New York Hist. Soc. 12-16-82	
	(1883) 1-13, 1-27	
	Duke University, Durham	
	(1893) 11-26, 12-2, 12-16	
Washington Tribune	District of Columbia, Wash-	1920
	ington	
	[Office of Publication:] 920 U	
	Street, NW	
	Issues on File: Library of Con-	
	gress 1921	
Watchman	Louisiana, Shreveport	1896
	Editor: S. H. Ralph	

Watchman	Tennessee, Memphis Editor: J. Thomas Turner Publisher: Watchman Publishing Co., 117 Beale Ave.	1878
Weekly Anglo-African	New York, New York Editor: Robert Hamilton Issues on File: Library of Congress 1865 West 135th Street Public Library of New York City (1865) 4-15, 5-6, 8-5, 10-14	1859

Weekly Defiance	Georgia, Atlanta
	    (Expired 1889)
	Issues on File: New York Public Library (1881) 10-8, 10-22, 10-29
	    New York Hist. Soc. 10-24-82, 2-24-83
		1881

Weekly Inquirer	New Jersey, Montclair· [Office of Publication:] 411 Orange Road	

Weekly Louisianian	Louisiana, New Orleans
	    (Expired 6-17-81)
	Issues on File: Library of Congress 1870; 1-25-78, 8-15-74; 3-27-75; 11-30-78; 6-17-82
	    Texas University, Austin 3-14-71, 2-28-74; 2-5-76; 9-29-77; 6-17-82
		12-18-1870

Weekly Loyal Georgian	Georgia, (?) Issue on File: Duke University, Durham 2-15-68	1866
Weekly Review	Iowa, Sioux City [Office of Publication:] 801 W. Eighth St., Sioux City, Iowa	
Western American (Followed by *Oakland Independent*)	California, Oakland (Expired 1929) Issues on File: Bancroft Library, University of California, Berkeley 11-14; 7-22-16, 10-22-21; (1922) 3-25, 4-22; (1926) 2-20, 3-5, 5-13, 8-21, 12-18; (1927) 1-1, 1-8, 2-12, 6-11, 12-10, 12-24; (1928) 1-21, 2-4, 2-18, 2-25, 3-10, 3-17, 4-14, 5	
*Western Ideal**	Colorado, Pueblo Publisher: M. O. Seymour, 100 W. First St.	1919

Western Messenger*	Missouri, Jefferson City (Expired 1917) Issues on File: Missouri Hist. Soc. 1-9-14 to 1917	1901
Western Optic	Missouri, Moberly Editor & Publisher: T. H. Phillips	1887
Western Outlook	California, Oakland (Expired 1928) Issues on File: Bancroft Library, University of California, Berkeley 11-14 to 7-22-16; 10-22-21; (1922) 3-25, 4-22; (1926) 2-20, 5-15, 6-12, 8-21, 12-18; (1927) 1-1, 1-8, 2-12, 6-11, 12-10, 12-24; (1928) 1-21, 2-4, 2-18, 2-25, 3-10, 3-17, 4-14, 5	1894
West Virginia Digest	West Virginia, Charleston Office of Publication: 910 East Washington St.	
Wichita Protest	Kansas, Wichita (Expired 1930) Issues on File: Kansas Hist. Soc., Topeka 6-19 to 10-19-23	1918
Wichita Tribune	Kansas, Wichita (Expired 1899) Issues on File: Kansas Hist. Soc., Topeka 7-23-98 to 99	1898
Wide Awake	Alabama, Birmingham (Expired 1900) Issues on File: Dept. of Archives and History, Montgomery 1-17-98 Library of Congress 1-24-00	1888
Wilmington Journal	North Carolina, Wilmington Editor: Thomas C. Jervay, 412 S. Seventh St.	1945
Wisconsin Enterprise	Wisconsin, Milwaukee [Office of Publication:] 1878 N. Ninth St.	
Wisconsin Enterprise Blade	Wisconsin, Milwaukee Editor: J. Anthony Josey	1916
Wisconsin Weekly	Wisconsin, Milwaukee (Expired 1915) Issues on File: Wisconsin State Hist. Soc., Madison, 1898 to 9-19-08	5-7-1898

Work	District of Columbia, Washington [Office of Publication:] 930 M Street, NW	
Wyandotte Echo	Kansas, Kansas City Editor: H. C. Chacey, 503 N. Sixth St.	1925

3

Additional Compilations

While working with Brown's checklist, errors became evident. In the following compilations, corrections appear in brackets; refer to Brown's list to determine change.

PLACE-OF-PUBLICATON INDEX

The following index was compiled from Brown's checklist by the author: a single date is the founding date; inclusive dates reflect the founding and expiring dates; no date indicates the dates are unknown.

ALABAMA

The Advance	Montgomery	1877–1882
Alabama Review	Montgomery	
Alabama Tribune	Montgomery	
American Press	Birmingham	1888–1895
Argus	Montgomery	1890
Birmingham Reporter	Birmingham	1902
Birmingham Review	Birmingham	1933
Birmingham World (Semi-weekly)	Birmingham	1931
Colored Alabamian	Tuscaloosa	1907–1916
Delta News	Mobile	1894
Emancipator	Montgomery	1917–1920
Enterprise	Montgomery	1898–1900
Gasden Call Post	Gasden	
Huntsville Gazette	Huntsville	1872–1894
Huntsville Gazette	Huntsville	1879
Huntsville Herald	Huntsville	1878–1883

Huntsville News	Huntsville	1917–1923
Huntsville Star	Huntsville	1900
Journal (1895–1896 as Huntsville Journal)	Huntsville	1895–1912
Journal	Huntsville	1895
Metropolitan Journal	Birmingham	1892
Mobile Weekly Press-Forum	Mobile	1894–1928
Negro Watchman	Montgomery	1874
New Idea	Selma	1891
People's Choice	Opelika	1894
Press	Mobile	1894
Reporter	Birmingham	1902
Southern Sentinel		1896–1899
Tuskegee Messenger	Tuskegee Institute	
Voice of the People		1913–1924
Wide Awake	Birmingham	1888–1900

ARIZONA

ARKANSAS

American Guide	Little Rock	1889
Arkansas Appreciator	Fort Smith	1896
Arkansas Baptist-Flashlight (Semi-monthly)	Fort Smith	1935
Arkansas Dispatch	Little Rock	1880–1896
Arkansas Freeman	Little Rock	1869–1871
Arkansas Herald	Little Rock	1882
Arkansas State Press	Little Rock	1941
Arkansas Survey	Little Rock	1923
Arkansas Survey-Journal	Little Rock	1934
Arkansas World	Little Rock	1940
Baptist Vanguard (Semi-monthly)	Little Rock	18__
Crystal	Hot Springs	1898
Echo	Pine Bluff	1889
Herald	Forrest City	1896
Hot Springs Echo	Hot Springs	
New Light	Forrest City	1899
Progress	Helena	1880

CALIFORNIA

Bay Cities Informer	Santa Monica	
California Eagle	Los Angeles	1879
California Voice	Oakland	1919
Criterion	Los Angeles	1942
Elevator	San Francisco	1865
Los Angeles Sentinel	Los Angeles	1932
Los Angeles Tribune	Los Angeles	1940
New Age-Dispatch	Los Angeles	1904

Oakland Independent (*Western American*)	Oakland	
Oakland Times	Oakland	1923
San Francisco Reporter	San Francisco	194_
San Francisco Sentinel	San Francisco	18__
Tri-County Bulletin	San Bernardino	1945
Vindicator	San Francisco	1884–1906
Western American (Followed by Oakland Independent)	Oakland	1929
Western Outlook	Oakland	1894–1928

COLORADO

Colorado Statesman	Denver	1894
Denver Star	Denver	
Statesman	Denver	1889
Voice of Colorado	Colorado Springs	
Western Ideal	Pueblo	1919

CONNECTICUT

Freeman's Chronicle	Hartford	1873
Hartford Advocate	Hartford	

DELAWARE

The Advance	Wilmington	1899–1901
Delaware Twilight	Wilmington	1886
New Era	Wilmington	1899

DISTRICT OF COLUMBIA

Afro-American	Washington	1892
Colored American	Washington	1893–1904
Commoner	Washington	1875
National Era	Washington	1847
New National Era	Washington	1869–1874
People's Advocate	Washington	1876–1886
Sentinel	Washington	1850
Sunday Item	Washington	1881
Washington American	Washington	1909
Washington Bee	Washington	1882–1922
Washington Tribune	Washington	1920
Work	Washington	

FLORIDA

The Advocate	Jacksonville	1891
Colored Citizen	Pensacola	1912
Florida Sentinel	Jacksonville	1887–1919
Florida Tattler	Jacksonville	
Miami Times	Miami	1923
Miami Whip	Miami	1943
Tampa Bulletin	Tampa	1915

GEORGIA

Afro-American Mouthpiece	Valdosta	1899
Age	Atlanta	1898
Athens Blade	Athens	1879–1880
Atlanta Age	Atlanta	1898–1908
Atlanta Daily World	Atlanta	1928
Atlanta Independent	Atlanta	
Augusta Union	Augusta	1889–1904
Blade	Eatonton	1894
Chronometer	Americus	1898
Clipper	Athens	1888
Colored American	August[a]	1865
Echo	Atlanta	
Echo	Griffin	1888
Echo	Savannah	1879
Enterprise	Rome	1903
Georgia Investigator	Americus	1899
Georgia Speaker	Atlanta	1895
Gleanor	Madison	1898
Independent	Atlanta	1903–1933
Journal	Savannah	1918
Loyal Georgian	Augusta	1866
Macon Sentinel	Macon	1899–1900
National Republican	Greenville	1898
People's Advocate	Atlanta	1891
Plain-Dealer	Valdosta	1898
Reporter	Atlanta	1895
Savannah Tribune	Savannah	1875
Savannah Weekly Echo	Savannah	1879
Sentinel	Augusta	1885
Southern Age	Atlanta	1891
Southern News	Savannah	18__
Tribune	Savannah	1886
Weekly Defiance	Atlanta	1881–1889
Weekly Loyal Georgian		1866

IDAHO

ILLINOIS

All About Us	Chicago	1896
Appeal	Chicago	1885–1923
Broadax	Chicago	1899–1919
The Cairo Gazette (Daily)	Cairo	1882–1882
Chicago Bee	Chicago	1909
Chicago Defender	Chicago	1909
Chicago Whip	Chicago	1919–1932
Chicago World	Chicago	1900
Church Organ	Chicago	1893

Clipper	Chicago	1885
Conservator	Chicago	1878
Egyptian Sun	Mound City	
Enterprise	Chicago	1918
Fellowship Herald	Chicago	1916
Free Lance	Chicago	1895–1926?
Free Speech	Chicago	1888
Illinois Conservator	Springfield	1905
Illinois Crusader	East Saint Louis	
Illinois Times	Champaign	1939
State Capital	Springfield	1886

INDIANA

Colored World	Indianapolis	1883
Courier	Indianapolis	1893
The Freeman	Indianapolis	1884–1926?
Gary American	Gary	1925
Indianapolis Recorder	Indianapolis	1897
Indianapolis World	Indianapolis	1883–1920
Lake County Observer	Gary	1946
Midwest Post	Indianapolis	
Public Ledger (Daily)	Baltimore	1887
Sunset Community Leader	Indianapolis	

IOWA

Avalanche	Des Moines	1891
Bystander	Des Moines	1894
Enterprise	Sioux City	
Iowa Observer	Des Moines	
Rising Sun	Des Moines	1883
Weekly Review	Sioux City	

KANSAS

American Citizen	Kansas City	1887–1909
American Citizen	Topeka	1888–1889
Call	Topeka	1891
Colored Citizen (Followed by Topeka Tribune)	Topeka	1878–1900
Colored Citizen	Wichita	1902–1904
Colored Patriot	Topeka	1882
Fair Play	Fort Scott	1898
Hutchinson Blade	Hutchinson	1914–1922
Kansas City Advocate	Kansas City	1914–1926
Kansas Elevator	Kansas City	1916–1918
Kansas Herald and Freedom	Lawrence	1855
Kansas State Ledger	Topeka	1892
Kansas Watchman	Topeka	1903–1905
Leavenworth Advocate	Leavenworth	1888–1891

National Reflector	Wichita	1895–1897?
Negro Star	Wichita	1908
People's Elevator	Independence	1924–1931
People's Elevator	Kansas City	1892
Plaindealer	Topeka	1899
Times Observer		1888–1892
Topeka Call	Topeka	1880–1898
Topeka Tribune	Topeka	1880–1881
Tribune	Wichita	1898
Wichita Protest	Wichita	1918–1930
Wichita Tribune	Wichita	1898–1899
Wyandotte Echo	Kansas City	1925

KENTUCKY

Bulletin	Louisville	1879
Independent	Ashland	
Indicator	Hopkinsville	1893
Informer	Louisville	1887
Kentucky Reporter	Louisville	1899
Lexington Standard	Lexington	1892–1912
Louisville Defender	Louisville	1933
Louisville Leader	Louisville	1917
Major	Hopkinsville	1897
New South	Louisville	1894
Ohio Falls Express	Louisville	1878–1904
Right House		1908
Standard	Lexington	1892
Sunday Unionist	Owensboro	1894

LOUISIANA

Black Republican	New Orleans	1865
Eagle Dispatch	Baton Rouge	
Ferret & Journal of the Lodge	New Orleans	1891
The Louisiana Daily (*New Orleans Semi-Weekly Louisianian* or *New Orleans Weekly Louisianian*)	New Orleans	1870–1888
Louisiana Republican	New Orleans	1881
Monitor	New Orleans	1893
Monitor	Donaldsonville	
National Negro Voice	New Orleans	1913–1916
Negro Gazette	New Orleans	1872
New Orleans Daily Creole	New Orleans	1857
New Orleans Sentinel	New Orleans	
Observer	Baton Rouge	1899–1900
Progressive Age	Alexandria	1897
Record	Shreveport	1896
Rescue	New Orleans	1893

Searchlight	Lake Charles	1898
Sepia Socialite (Changed to *The Negro South,* monthly magazine, Jan. 1946)	New Orleans	1936
Shreveport Sun	Shreveport	1920
La Tribune de la Nouvelle-Orleans (Daily)	New Orleans	1864–1870
Union (L'Union) (In French and English)	New Orleans	1862
Vindicator	New Orleans	18__
Watchman	Shreveport	1896
Weekly Louisianian	New Orleans	1870–1881

MAINE

MARYLAND

Afro-American (1901–1916 as *Afro-American Ledger,* semi-weekly)	Baltimore	1892
American-Citizen	Baltimore	1879
Crusader	Baltimore	1893
Herald-Commonwealth	Baltimore	1920–193_
Negro Appeal	Annapolis	1899–1900
Race Standard	Baltimore	1894–1898
Signal	Cumberland	1897

MASSACHUSETTS

Boston Courant	Boston	1890
Cambridge Mirror	Cambridge	1906–1909
Chronicle	Boston	1916
Emancipator and Free American	Boston	1842–1844
Guardian	Boston	1901

MICHIGAN

Detroit Contender	Detroit	1920–1921
Detroit Informer	Detroit	1897–1916
Detroit Tribune	Detroit	1922
Independent	Detroit	1922
Michigan Chronicle	Detroit	1936
Michigan Independent (1922–1935 as *Independent;* 1935 as *Northwestern News*)		1922
Michigan State News	Grand Rapids	1920–1925
National Independent	Detroit	1891

MINNESOTA

Afro-American	Minneapolis	1899–1905?
Afro-Independent	St. Paul	1888

Minneapolis Spokesman	Minneapolis	1934
St. Paul Recorder	St. Paul	1934
Twin City Observer	Minneapolis	1943

MISSISSIPPI

The Advance Dispatch	Mound Bayou	1914–1933
Brotherhood	Natchez	1887
Light	Vicksburg	1891–1895
People's Defender	Jackson	1889–1895
Reporter	Natchez	1909

MISSOURI

The Advance	St. Louis	1882
American Eagle	St. Louis	1894–1907
Call	Kansas City	1919
Christian Advocate	Kansas City	
Contributor	St. Louis	1883
Kansas City American	Kansas City	1928
Kansas City Observer	Kansas City	1896–1901
Kansas City Sun	Kansas City	1908–1924
Liberator	Kansas City	1901
Mirror	St. Joseph	1886
Observer	Kansas City	1896
Palladium	St. Louis	1899
Radical	St. Joseph	1897
Register	Hannibal	1919
Rising Sun	Kansas City	1896–1918
St. Louis American	St. Louis	1928
St. Louis Argus	St. Louis	1912
St. Louis Clarion	St. Louis	1915–1922
St. Louis Recorder	St. Louis	1943
Sedalia Times	Sedalia	1894–1905
Times	Sedalia	1894–1905?
(Same as *Sedalia Times*)		
Western Optic	Moberly	1887
Western Messenger	Jefferson City	1901–1917

MONTANA

NEBRASKA

Afro-American Sentinel	Omaha	1893–1911
Enterprise	Omaha	1893–1914
Omaha Guide	Omaha	1927
Omaha Monitor	Omaha	1915–1929
Progress	Omaha	1889–1904

NEVADA

NEW HAMPSHIRE

NEW JERSEY

Afro-American	Newark	
New Jersey Herald Guardian	Newark	
New Jersey Herald News	Newark	1927
New Jersey Record	Newark	1934
New Jersey Trumpet	Newark	1887
North Jersey News	Montclair	
Weekly Inquirer	Montclair	

NEW MEXICO

NEW YORK

The Advocate	Buffalo	1923
Albany Enterprise	Albany	
Amsterdam News (Later: *Amsterdam Star News*, 1941)	New York	1909
Associated Negro News	New York	
Buffalo Broadcaster	Buffalo	
Buffalo Criterion	Buffalo	1934
Buffalo Spokesman	Buffalo	
Buffalo Star	Buffalo	1932
Capitol	Albany	1894
Colored American (Also *Weekly Advocate*)	New York	1837–1842
The Colored Man's Journal	New York	1851–1856
Ethiopian World (*Negro World*, 1917–1933; *World Peace Echo*, 1921–1934)	New York	1917–1934
Frederick Douglass' Paper (1847–1851 as *North Star*)	Rochester	1847–1863
Freedom's Journal (Also known as *Rights of All*)	New York	1827–1830
Globe	New York	1880–1884
Jamaica Gleaner	Long Island	
The Listener	Bronx	
Negro World (Daily/weekly)	New York	1919–1933
New York Age (188[0]–1884 *New York Globe; Freeman* 1884; *New York Freeman* 1883)	New York	1880
New York News	New York	1913–193_
The People's Voice	New York	1942
Progressive Herald	Syracuse	1933
Ram's Horn	New York	1847–1848

Republican	New York	1896
Rights of All (Formerly *Freedom's Journal*)	New York	
Rochester Voice (See *Voice Newspaper*)	Rochester	1933
Voice of Ethiopia	New York	
Voice Newspaper (See *Rochester Voice*)	Rochester	
Weekly Anglo-African	New York	1859

NORTH CAROLINA

Banner	Raleigh	1881
Cape Fear Journal	Wilmington	
Carolina Enterprise	Goldsboro	1881
Carolina Times	Durham	
Carolina Tribune	Raleigh	1926
Carolinian	Raleigh	1920
Charlotte Post	Charlotte	
The Democrat	Greensboro	
Gazette	Raleigh	1883–1897
Greensboro North Carolina Patriot	Greensboro	
Post	Charlotte	1926
Record	Asheville	
Southern News	Asheville	
True Reformer	Littleton	1889
Wilmington Journal	Wilmington	1945

NORTH DAKOTA

OHIO

Afro-American	Cincinnati	1882
The Alienated American	Cleveland	1851–1856
Buckeye Review	Youngstown	1938
Cleveland Advocate	Cleveland	1914–1923
Cleveland Call and Post	Cleveland	1921
Cleveland Guide	Cleveland	1931
Cleveland Herald	Cleveland	1938
Colored Citizen	Cincinnati	1863–1869
Columbus Messenger	Columbus	1887
Columbus Voice	Columbus	1883
Daily Bulletin	Dayton	1941
Daily Express	Dayton	1942
Dayton Forum	Dayton	1913
Forum [Same as *Dayton Forum*?]	Dayton	1913
Gazette	Cleveland	1883
Ohio Express	Springfield	
Ohio Republican	Cincinnati	1884
Ohio State News	Columbus	1942

Ohio State Tribune	Springfield	1884
Union	Cincinnati	1907–1923?

OKLAHOMA

Ardmore Sun	Ardmore	1901–1911
Black Dispatch	Oklahoma City	1915
Daily Search Light	Muskogee	1905–1906
Muskogee Lantern (Expired 1926 as *Watchman and Lantern*)	Muskogee	1922–1926
Muskogee Republican	Muskogee	1905–1912?
Muskogee Star	Muskogee	1912
Oklahoma Eagle	Tulsa	1922
Oklahoma Independent	Muskogee	

OREGON

The Advocate	Portland	1907–1933?

PENNSYLVANIA

Afro-American	Philadelphia	1892
Afro Dispatch	Pittsburgh	
Broad Axe	Pittsburgh	1896
Crusader	Pittsburgh	
Defender	Philadelphia	1897
Journal	Pittsburgh	1893
Philadelphia Independent	Philadelphia	1931
Philadelphia Tribune	Philadelphia	1884
Pittsburgh Courier	Pittsburgh	1907
Pittsburgh Examiner	Pittsburgh	
Southwestern Christian Advocate	Philadelphia	18__
Standard Echo	Philadelphia	1881

RHODE ISLAND

The Advance	Providence	1906–1914

SOUTH CAROLINA

Afro-American Citizen	Charleston	1899–1900
Charlestown Journal	Charlestown	1866
Free Press	Charleston	1868
Georgetown Planet Weekly	Georgetown	1873
Lighthouse and Informer	Columbia	1937
Messenger	Charleston	1894
Missionary Record	Charleston	1871
Palmetto Leader	Columbia	1925
South Carolina Leader	Charleston	1865–1868

SOUTH DAKOTA

TENNESSEE

Colored Tennessean	Nashville	1866–1867
Defender	Chattanooga	1917
East Tennessee News	Knoxville	1906
Flashlight Herald	Knoxville	1931
Herald	Knoxville	1927
Index	Memphis	1923
Knoxville Negro World (Daily)	Knoxville	1887
Memphis Journal	Memphis	
Memphis World (Semi-weekly)	Memphis	1931
Nashville Globe (*Globe Independent*)	Nashville	1906
Negro Journal of Industry	Memphis	
Negro World	Knoxville	1887–1895
Southern American	Chattanooga	1884
Tennessee Star	[?]	1886–1891
Watchman	Memphis	1878

TEXAS

City Times	Galveston	1898–1930
Clarion	Waco	1921
Colored American	Galveston	1920–1925
Dallas Express	Dallas	1893–1894
Echo	Beaumont	1893
Fort Worth Peoples Contender	Fort Worth	
Herald	Austin	1890–1930?
Houston Defender	Houston	1930
Houston Freeman	Houston	1893
Houston Informer (1931–1934 as *Houston Informer & Texas Freeman*)	Houston	1919
Houston Observer	Houston	1916–1921
Houston Sentinel	Houston	1927–1931
Industrial Era	Beaumont	1903
Item	Dallas	18__
Item	Fort Worth	1890
Messenger	Waco	1932
Mind	Fort Worth	1931
Negro Labor News	Houston	1931
Register	San Antonio	1931
San Antonio Inquirer	San Antonio	
San Antonio Register	San Antonio	1931
Texas Examiner	Houston	1942
Texas Headlight	Austin	1895

UTAH

VERMONT

VIRGINIA

The Advance	Norfolk	1893–1894
Afro-American	Richmond	1939
American Ethiopia	Norfolk	1903?–1907?
American Problem	Hampton	1905–1911
American Sentinel	Petersburg	1880–1881
Caret	Newport News	1895
Enterprise	Pulaski	1908–1916
Evening Recorder	Newport News	1893
Herald	Petersburg	1888
Industrial Day	Richmond	1888–1890?
Interpreter	Lynchburg	1903–1906
Journal and Guide	Norfolk	1901
Laboring Man	Lynchburg	1886–1887?
Leader	Alexandria	1888–1900
Negro Criterion	Richmond	1905–1909
Newport News Post	Newport News	
Newport News Star (Succeeds Evening Recorder)	Newport News	1901
People's Light	Pulaski	1893
Petersburg Herald	Petersburg	188_–1889
Press	Port Royal	1893–1898
Press	Roanoke	1891–1897
Recorder	Norfolk	1893
The Reformer	Richmond	1895–1931
Reporter	Richmond	1890–1893
Review	Petersburg	–1925
Richmond Planet	Richmond	1883
Southern News	Richmond	1890–1894
Standard	Norfolk	1889–1891
Star	Newport News	1903
Tribune	Staunton	19__–1933
Valley Index	Staunton	1897–1905
Virginia Star	Richmond	1877–1888
Voice	Richmond	1918–1925

WASHINGTON

Northwest Enterprise	Seattle	1920
Northwest Herald	Seattle	1935
Seattle Republican	Seattle	1894–1915

WEST VIRGINIA

Color	Charleston	1943
McDowell Times	Keystone	1913
Messenger	Charleston	
West Virginia Digest	Charleston	

WISCONSIN

Northwestern Recorder	Milwaukee	1892–1893
(4/1892–11/1892 as *Wisconsin Afro-American*)		
Wisconsin Enterprise	Milwaukee	
Wisconsin Enterprise Blade	Milwaukee	1916
Wisconsin Weekly	Milwaukee	1898–1915

WYOMING

YEAR-OF-PUBLICATION INDEX

The day and/or month are as presented in Brown's checklist.

3-16-1827	*Freedom's Journal**	New York, N.Y.
1837	*Colored American**	New York, N.Y.
1842	*Emancipator and Free American*	Boston, Mass.
12-3-1847	*Frederick Douglass' Paper**	Rochester, N.Y.
1847	*National Era*	Washington, D.C.
1847	*Ram's Horn*	New York, N.Y.
1850	*Sentinel*	Washington, D.C.
1851	*The Alienated American*	Cleveland, Ohio
1851	*The Colored Man's Journal*	New York, N.Y.
1855	*Kansas Herald and Freedom*	Lawrence
1857	*New Orleans Daily Creole*	La.
1859	*Weekly Anglo-African*	New York, N.Y.
1862	*Union (L'Union)*	New Orleans, La.
1863	*Colored Citizen*	Cincinnati, Ohio
1864	*La Tribune de La Nouvelle-Orleans*	La.
4-6-1865	*Elevator*	San Francisco, Calif.
4-15-1865	*Black Republican*	New Orleans, La.
12-16-1865	*Colored American*	August[a], Ga.
1865	*South Carolina Leader*	Charleston
3-24-1866	*Colored Tennessean*	Nashville
1866	*Charlestown Journal*	S.C.
1866	*Loyal Georgian*	Augusta
1866	*Weekly Loyal Georgian*	(?)
1868	*Free Press*	Charleston, S.C.

*Indicates a second title or merger.

8-24-1869	*Arkansas Freeman*	Little Rock
1869	*New National Era*	Washington, D.C.
12-18-1870	*Weekly Louisianian*	New Orleans
1871	*Missionary Record*	Charleston, S.C.
9-18-1872	*Negro Gazette*	New Orleans, La.
11-22-1872	*Huntsville Gazette*	Ala.
1873	*Freeman's Chronicle*	Hartford, Conn.
1873	*Georgetown Planet Weekly*	S.C.
1874	*Negro Watchman*	Montgomery, Ala.
1875	*Commoner*	Washington, D.C.
1875	*Savannah Tribune*	Ga.
1876	*People's Advocate*	Washington, D.C.
4-1877	*Virginia Star*	Richmond
1877	*The Advance*	Montgomery, Ala.
1878	*Colored Citizen**	Topeka, Kans.
1878	*Conservator*	Chicago, Ill.
1878	*Huntsville Herald*	Ala.
1878	*Ohio Falls Express*	Louisville, Ky.
1878	*Watchman*	Memphis, Tenn.
4-8-1879	*California Eagle*	Los Angeles
8-1879	*American-Citizen*	Baltimore, Md.
1879	*Athens Blade*	Ga.
1879	*Bulletin*	Louisville, Ky.
1879	*Echo*	Savannah, Ga.
1879	*Huntsville Gazette*	Ala.
1879	*Savannah Weekly Echo*	Ga.
1880	*American Sentinel*	Petersburg, Va.
1880	*Arkansas Dispatch*	Little Rock
1880	*Globe*	New York, N.Y.
1880	*New York Age**	N.Y.
1880	*Progress*	Helena, Ark.
1880	*Topeka Call*	Kans.
1880	*Topeka Tribune*	Kans.
1881	*Banner*	Raleigh, N.C.
1881	*Carolina Enterprise*	Goldsboro, N.C.
1881	*Louisiana Republican*	New Orleans
1881	*Standard Echo*	Philadelphia, Pa.
1881	*Sunday Item*	Washington, D.C.
1881	*Weekly Defiance*	Atlanta, Ga.
1-3-1882	*Washington Bee**	D.C.
4-23-1882	*The Cairo Gazette*	Ill.
1882	*The Advance*	St. Louis, Mo.
1882	*Afro-American*	Cincinnati, Ohio
1882	*Arkansas Herald*	Little Rock
1882	*Colored Patriot*	Topeka, Kans.
8-25-1883	*Gazette*	Cleveland, Ohio

1883	*Colored World*	Indianapolis, Ind.
1883	*Columbus Voice*	Ohio
1883	*Contributor*	St. Louis, Mo.
1883	*Gazette*	Raleigh, N.C.
1883	*Indianapolis World*	Ind.
1883	*Richmond Planet*	Va.
1883	*Rising Sun*	Des Moines, Iowa
1884	*The Freeman*	Indianapolis, Ind.
1884	*Ohio Republican*	Cincinnati
1884	*Ohio State Tribune*	Springfield
1884	*Philadelphia Tribune*	Pa.
1884	*Southern American*	Chattanooga, Tenn.
1884	*Vindicator*	San Francisco, Calif.
1885	*Appeal**	Chicago, Ill.
1885	*Clipper*	Chicago, Ill.
1885	*Sentinel*	Augusta, Ga.
1886	*Delaware Twilight*	Wilmington
1886	*Laboring Man**	Lynchburg, Va.
1886	*Mirror*	St. Joseph, Mo.
1886	*State Capital*	Springfield, Ill.
1886	*Tennessee Star*	(?)
1886	*Tribune*	Savannah, Ga.
11-17-1887	*Negro World*	Knoxville, Tenn.
1887	*American Citizen*	Kansas City, Kans.
1887	*Brotherhood*	Natchez, Miss.
1887	*Columbus Messenger*	Ohio
1887	*Florida Sentinel*	Jacksonville
1887	*Informer*	Louisville, Ky.
1887	*Knoxville Negro World*	Tenn.
1887	*New Jersey Trumpet*	Newark
1887	*Public Ledger*	Baltimore, Ind.
1887	*Western Optic*	Moberly, Mo.
7-9-1888	*Afro-Independent*	St. Paul, Minn.
1888	*American Citizen*	Topeka, Kans.
1888	*American Press*	Birmingham, Ala.
1888	*Clipper*	Athens, Ga.
1888	*Echo*	Griffin, Ga.
1888	*Free Speech*	Chicago, Ill.
1888	*Herald*	Petersburg, Va.
1888	*Industrial Day*	Richmond, Va.
1888	*Leader**	Alexandria, Va.
1888	*Leavenworth Advocate*	Kans.
1888	*Times Observer*	Kans.
1888	*Wide Awake*	Birmingham, Ala.
1889	*American Guide*	Little Rock, Ark.
1889	*Augusta Union*	Ga.
1889	*Echo*	Pine Bluff, Ark.
1889	*People's Defender*	Jackson, Miss.

1889	*Progress*	Omaha, Nebr.
1889	*Standard*	Norfolk, Va.
1889	*Statesman*	Denver, Colo.
1890	*Argus*	Montgomery, Ala.
1890	*Boston Courant*	Mass.
1890	*Herald*	Austin, Tex.
1890	*Item*	Fort Worth, Tex.
1890	*Reporter*	Richmond, Va.
1890	*Southern News*	Richmond, Va.
1891	*The Advocate*	Jacksonville, Fla.
1891	*Avalanche*	Des Moines, Iowa
1891	*Call*	Topeka, Kans.
1891	*Ferret & Journal of the Lodge*	New Orleans, La.
1891	*Light*	Vicksburg, Miss.
1891	*National Independent*	Detroit, Mich.
1891	*New Idea*	Selma, Ala.
1891	*People's Advocate*	Atlanta, Ga.
1891	*Press*	Roanoke, Va.
1891	*Southern Age*	Atlanta, Ga.
4-1892	*Northwestern Recorder**	Milwaukee, Wisc.
1892	*Afro-American**	Baltimore, Md.
1892	*Afro-American*	Philadelphia, Pa.
1892	*Afro-American*	Washington, D.C.
1892	*Kansas State Ledger*	Topeka
1892	*Lexington Standard*	Ky.
1892	*Metropolitan Journal*	Birmingham, Ala.
1892	*People's Elevator*	Independence, Kans.
1892	*Standard*	Lexington, Ky.
1-1893	*Enterprise*	Omaha, Nebr.
1893	*The Advance*	Norfolk, Va.
1893	*Afro-American Sentinel*	Omaha, Nebr.
1893	*Church Organ*	Chicago, Ill.
1893	*Colored American*	Washington, D.C.
1893	*Courier*	Indianapolis, Ind.
1893	*Crusader*	Baltimore, Md.
1893	*Dallas Express*	Tex.
1893	*Echo*	Beaumont, Tex.
1893	*Evening Recorder**	Newport News, Va.
1893	*Houston Freeman*	Tex.
1893	*Indicator*	Hopkinsville, Ky.
1893	*Journal*	Pittsburg, Pa.
1893	*Monitor*	New Orleans, La.
1893	*People's Light*	Pulaski, Va.
1893	*Press*	Port Royal, Va.
1893	*Recorder*	Norfolk, Va.
1893	*Rescue*	New Orleans, La.
1894	*American Eagle*	St. Louis, Mo.

1894	*Blade*	Eatonton, Ga.
1894	*Bystander**	Des Moines, Iowa
1894	*Capitol*	Albany, N.Y.
1894	*Colorado Statesman*	Denver
1894	*Delta News*	Mobile, Ala.
1894	*Messenger*	Charleston, S.C.
1894	*Mobile Weekly Press-Forum*	Ala.
1894	*New South*	Louisville, Ky.
1894	*People's Choice*	Opelika, Ala.
1894	*Press*	Mobile, Ala.
1894	*Race Standard*	Baltimore, Md.
1894	*Seattle Republican*	Wash.
1894	*Sedalia Times*	Mo.
1894	*Sunday Unionist*	Owensboro, Ky.
1894	*Times*	Sedalia, Mo.
1894	*Western Outlook*	Oakland, Calif.
1895	*Caret*	Newport News, Va.
1895	*Free Lance*	Chicago, Ill.
1895	*Georgia Speaker*	Atlanta
1895	*Journal** (as *Huntsville Journal*)	Huntsville, Ala.
1895	*Journal*	Huntsville, Ala.
1895	*National Reflector*	Wichita, Kans.
1895	*The Reformer*	Richmond, Va.
1895	*Reporter*	Atlanta, Ga.
1895	*Texas Headlight*	Austin
1896	*All About Us*	Chicago, Ill.
1896	*Arkansas Appreciator*	Fort Smith
1896	*Broad Axe*	Pittsburgh, Pa.
1896	*Herald*	Forrest City, Ark.
1896	*Kansas City Observer*	Mo.
1896	*Observer*	Kansas City, Mo.
1896	*Record*	Shreveport, La.
1896	*Republican*	New York, N.Y.
1896	*Rising Sun*	Kansas City, Mo.
1896	*Southern Sentinel*	Ala.
1896	*Watchman*	Shreveport, La.
1897	*Defender*	Philadelphia, Pa.
1897	*Detroit Informer*	Mich.
1897	*Indianapolis Recorder*	Ind.
1897	*Major*	Hopkinsville, Ky.
1897	*Progressive Age*	Alexandria, La.
1897	*Radical*	St. Joseph, Mo.
1897	*Signal*	Cumberland, Md.
1897	*Valley Index*	Staunton, Va.
5-7-1898	*Wisconsin Weekly*	Milwaukee
1898	*Age*	Atlanta, Ga.
1898	*Atlanta Age*	Ga.
1898	*Chronometer*	Americus, Ga.

1898	*City Times*	Galveston, Tex.
1898	*Crystal*	Hot Springs, Ark.
1898	*Enterprise*	Montgomery, Ala.
1898	*Fair Play*	Fort Scott, Kans.
1898	*Gleanor*	Madison, Ga.
1898	*National Republican*	Greensville, Ga.
1898	*Plain-Dealer*	Valdosta, Ga.
1898	*Searchlight*	Lake Charles, La.
1898	*Tribune*	Wichita, Kans.
1898	*Wichita Tribune*	Kans.
5-27-1899	*Afro-American*	Minneapolis, Minn.
1899	*The Advance*	Wilmington, Del.
1899	*Afro-American Citizen*	Charleston, S.C.
1899	*Afro-American Mouthpiece*	Valdosta, Ga.
1899	*Broadax*	Chicago, Ill.
1899	*Georgia Investigator*	Americus
1899	*Kentucky Reporter*	Louisville
1899	*Macon Sentinel*	Ga.
1899	*Negro Appeal*	Annapolis, Md.
1899	*New Era*	Wilmington, Del.
1899	*New Light*	Forrest City, Ark.
1899	*Observer*	Baton Rouge, La.
1899	*Palladium*	St. Louis, Mo.
1899	*Plaindealer*	Topeka, Kans.
1899	*True Reformer*	Littleton, N.C.
1-26-1900	*Huntsville Star*	Ala.
1900	*Chicago World*	Ill.
2-1901	*Liberator*	Kansas City, Mo.
1901	*Ardmore Sun**	Okla.
1901	*Guardian*	Boston, Mass.
1901	*Journal and Guide*	Norfolk, Va.
1901	*Newport News Star**	Va.
1901	*Western Messenger*	Jefferson City, Mo.
1902	*Birmingham Reporter*	Ala.
1902	*Colored Citizen*	Wichita, Kans.
1902	*Muskogee Lantern**	Okla.
1902	*Reporter*	Birmingham, Ala.
1903(?)	*American Ethiopia*	Norfolk, Va.
1903	*Enterprise*	Rome, Ga.
1903	*Independent*	Atlanta, Ga.
1903	*Industrial Era*	Beaumont, Tex.
1903	*Interpreter*	Lynchburg, Va.
1903	*Kansas Watchman*	Topeka
1903	*Star*	Newport News, Va.
1904	*New Age-Dispatch*	Los Angeles, Calif.
1905	*American Problem*	Hampton, Va.
1905	*Chicago Defender*	Ill.

1905	*Daily Search Light*	Muskogee, Okla.
1905	*Illinois Conservator*	Springfield
1905	*Muskogee Republican*	Okla.
1905	*Negro Criterion*	Richmond, Va.
7-6-1906	*The Advance*	Providence, R.I.
1906	*Cambridge Mirror*	Mass.
1906	*East Tennessee News*	Knoxville
1906	*Nashville Globe**	Tenn.
3-1907	*The Advocate*	Portland, Oreg.
1907	*Colored Alabamian*	Tuscaloosa, Ala.
1907	*Pittsburgh Courier*	Pa.
1907	*Union*	Cincinnati, Ohio
1908	*Enterprise*	Pulaski, Va.
1908	*Kansas City Sun*	Mo.
1908	*Negro Star*	Wichita, Kans.
1908	*Right House*	Ky.
1-1909	*Washington American*	D.C.
1909	*Amsterdam News**	New York, N.Y.
1909	*Chicago Bee*	Ill.
1909	*Reporter*	Natchez, Miss.
1912	*Colored Citizen*	Pensacola, Fla.
1912	*Muskogee Star*	Okla.
1912	*St. Louis Argus*	Mo.
5-16-1913	*Dayton Forum*	Ohio
12-16-1913	*National Negro Voice*	New Orleans, La.
1913	*Forum*	Dayton, Ohio
1913	*McDowell Times*	Keystone, W.V.
1913	*New York News*	N.Y.
1913	*Voice of the People*	Ala.
1914	*The Advance Dispatch*	Mound Bayou, Miss.
1914	*Cleveland Advocate*	Ohio
1914	*Hutchinson Blade*	Kans.
1914	*Kansas City Advocate*	Kans.
7-3-1915	*Omaha Monitor*	Nebr.
1915	*Black Dispatch*	Oklahoma City, Okla.
1915	*St. Louis Clarion*	Mo.
1915	*Tampa Bulletin*	Fla.
1916	*Chronicle*	Boston, Mass.
1916	*Fellowship Herald*	Chicago, Ill.
1916	*Houston Observer*	Tex.
1916	*Kansas Elevator*	Kansas City
1916	*Wisconsin Enterprise Blade*	Milwaukee
1917	*Defender*	Chattanooga, Tenn.
1917	*Emancipator*	Montgomery, Ala.
1917	*Ethiopian World**	New York, N.Y.
1917	*Huntsville News*	Ala.
1917	*Louisville Leader*	Ky.

1918	*Enterprise*	Chicago, Ill.
1918	*Journal*	Savannah, Ga.
1918	*Voice*	Richmond, Va.
1918	*Wichita Protest*	Kans.
5-24-1919	*Houston Informer**	Tex.
1919	*California Voice*	Oakland
1919	*Call*	Kansas City, Mo.
1919	*Chicago Whip*	Ill.
1919	*Negro World*	New York, N.Y.
1919	*Register*	Hannibal, Mo.
1919	*Western Ideal*	Pueblo, Colo.
10-6-1920	*Shreveport Sun*	La.
1920	*Carolinian*	Raleigh, N.C.
1920	*Colored American*	Galveston, Tex.
1920	*Detroit Contender*	Mich.
1920	*Herald-Commonwealth*	Baltimore, Md.
1920	*Michigan State News*	Grand Rapids
1920	*Northwest Enterprise*	Seattle, Wash.
1920	*Washington Tribune*	D.C.
2-22-1921	*Cleveland Call and Post*	Ohio
1921	*Clarion*	Waco, Tex.
1922	*Detroit Tribune*	Mich.
1922	*Independent*	Detroit, Mich.
1922	*Michigan Independent**	(?)
1922	*Oklahoma Eagle*	Tulsa
9-29-1923	*Oakland Times*	Calif.
1923	*The Advocate*	Buffalo, N.Y.
1923	*Arkansas Survey*	Little Rock
1923	*Index*	Memphis, Tenn.
1923	*Miami Times*	Fla.
1924	*People's Elevator*	Kansas City, Kans.
1925	*Gary American*	Ind.
1925	*Palmetto Leader*	Columbia, S.C.
1925	*Wyandotte Echo*	Kans.
1926	*Carolina Tribune*	Raleigh, N.C.
1926	*Post*	Charlotte, N.C.
1927	*Herald*	Knoxville, Tenn.
1927	*Houston Sentinel*	Tex.
1927	*New Jersey Herald News*	Newark
1927	*Omaha Guide*	Nebr.
4-12-1928	*Kansas City American*	Mo.
1928	*Atlanta Daily World*	Ga.
1928	*St. Louis American*	Mo.
10-11-1930	*Houston Defender*	Tex.
1931	*Birmingham World*	Ala.
1931	*Cleveland Guide*	Ohio

1931	*Flashlight Herald*	Knoxville, Tenn.
1931	*Memphis World*	Tenn.
1931	*Mind*	Fort Worth, Tex.
1931	*Negro Labor News*	Houston, Tex.
1931	*Philadelphia Independent*	Pa.
1931	*Register*	San Antonio, Tex.
1931	*San Antonio Register*	Tex.
1932	*Buffalo Star*	N.Y.
1932	*Los Angeles Sentinel*	Calif.
1932	*Messenger*	Waco, Tex.
1933	*Birmingham Review*	Ala.
1933	*Louisville Defender*	Ky.
1933	*Progressive Herald*	Syracuse, N.Y.
1933	*Rochester Voice*	N.Y.
1934	*Arkansas Survey-Journal*	Little Rock
1934	*Buffalo Criterion*	N.Y.
1934	*Minneapolis Spokesman*	Minn.
1934	*New Jersey Record*	Newark
1934	*St. Paul Recorder*	Minn.
1935	*Arkansas Baptist Flashlight*	Fort Smith
1935	*Northwest Herald*	Seattle, Wash.
1936	*Michigan Chronicle*	Detroit
1936	*Sepia Socialite**	New Orleans, La.
1937	*Lighthouse and Informer*	Columbia, S.C.
1938	*Buckeye Review*	Youngstown, Ohio
1938	*Cleveland Herald*	Ohio
1939	*Afro-American*	Richmond, Va.
1939	*Illinois Times*	Champaign
1940	*Arkansas World*	Little Rock
1940	*Los Angeles Tribune*	Calif.
1941	*Arkansas State Press*	Little Rock
1941	*Daily Bulletin*	Dayton, Ohio
1942	*Criterion*	Los Angeles, Calif.
1942	*Daily Express*	Dayton, Ohio
1942	*Ohio State News*	Columbus
1942	*The People's Voice*	New York, N.Y.
1942	*Texas Examiner*	Houston
1943	*Color*	Charleston, W.V.
1943	*Miami Whip*	Fla.
1943	*St. Louis Recorder*	Mo.
1943	*Twin City Observer*	Minneapolis, Minn.
1945	*Tri-County Bulletin*	San Bernardino, Calif.
1945	*Wilmington Journal*	N.C.
1946	*Lake County Observer*	Gary, Ind.

UNDATED PUBLICATIONS INDEX

Afro-American	Newark, N.J.	
Afro Dispatch	Pittsburgh, Pa.	
Alabama Review	Montgomery	
Alabama Tribune	Montgomery	
Albany Enterprise	N.Y.	
Associated Negro News	New York, N.Y.	
Atlanta Independent	Ga.	
Baptist Vanguard	Little Rock, Ark.	18__
Bay Cities Informer	Santa Monica, Calif.	
Buffalo Broadcaster	N.Y.	
Buffalo Spokesman	N.Y.	
Cape Fear Journal	Wilmington, N.C.	
Carolina Times	Durham, N.C.	
Charlotte Post	N.C.	
Christian Advocate	Kansas City, Mo.	
Crusader	Pittsburgh, Pa.	
The Democrat	Greensboro, N.C.	
Denver Star	Colo.	
Eagle Dispatch	Baton Rouge, La.	
Echo	Atlanta, Ga.	
Egyptian Sun	Mound City, Ill.	
Enterprise	Sioux City, Iowa	
Florida Tattler	Jacksonville	
Fort Worth Peoples Contender	Tex.	
Gasden Call Post	Ala.	
Greensboro North Carolina Patriot		
Hartford Advocate	Conn.	
Hot Springs Echo	Ark.	
Illinois Crusader	East St. Louis	
Independent	Ashland, Ky.	
Iowa Observer	Des Moines	
Item	Dallas, Tex.	18__?
Jamaica Gleaner	Long Island, N.Y.	
Listener	Bronx, N.Y.	
Memphis Journal	Tenn.	
Messenger	Charleston, W.V.	
Midwest Post	Indianapolis, Ind.	
Monitor	Donaldsonville, La.	
Negro Journal of Industry	Memphis, Tenn.	
New Jersey Herald Guardian	Newark	
New Orleans Sentinel	La.	
Newport News Post	Va.	
North Jersey News	Montclair, N.J.	

Oakland Independent (*Western American*)	Calif.	
Ohio Express	Springfield	
Oklahoma Independent	Muskogee	
Petersburg Herald	Va.	188_?
Pittsburgh Examiner	Pa.	
Record	Asheville, N.C.	
Review	Petersburg, Va.	
San Antonio Inquirer	Tex.	
San Francisco Reporter	Calif.	194_
San Francisco Sentinel	Calif.	18_
Southern News	Asheville, N.C.	
Southern News	Savannah, Ga.	18_
Southwestern Christian Advocate	Philadelphia, Pa.	18_
Sunset Community Leader	Indianapolis, Ind.	
Tribune	Staunton, Va.	19_
Tuskegee Messenger	Tuskegee Institute, Ala.	
Vindicator	New Orleans, La.	18_
Voice of Colorado	Colorado Springs	
Voice of Ethiopia	New York, N.Y.	
Voice Newspaper	Rochester, N.Y.	
Weekly Inquirer	Montclair, N.J.	
Weekly Review	Sioux City, Iowa	
West Virginia Digest	Charleston	
Wisconsin Enterprise	Milwaukee	
Work	Washington, D.C.	

EDITOR INDEX

Adams, J. Victor	*Enterprise*	Pulaski, Va.
Adams, John Wesley	*Public Ledger*	Baltimore, Ind.
Adams, O. W.	*Reporter*	Birmingham, Ala.
Andrews, U. J.	*San Antonio Register*	Tex.
Andrews, W. T.	*Herald-Commonwealth*	Baltimore, Md.
Astwood, H. C. C.	*Defender*	Philadelphia, Pa.
Atwater, A. T.	*Enterprise*	Rome, Ga.
Bailey, J. T.	*Arkansas Herald*	Little Rock
Banks, A. C.	*Major*	Hopkinsville, Ky.
Barnett, F. L.	*Conservator*	Chicago, Ill.
Bass, Charlotta A.	*California Eagle*	Los Angeles
Bates, L. C.	*Arkansas State Press*	Little Rock
Benjamin, R. C. O.	*San Francisco Sentinel*	Calif.
Bennett, J. R.	*Crystal*	Hot Springs, Ark.

Berry, R. T.	*Kentucky Reporter*	Louisville
Binford, H. C.	*Journal*	Huntsville, Ala.
Bolton, Rev. L. V.	*Texas Examiner*	Houston
Boughman, Theo.	*Oklahoma Eagle*	Tulsa
Bowley, James A./R. O. Bush	*Georgetown Planet Weekly*	S.C.
Boyd, Peter	*Indicator*	Hopkinsville, Ky.
Boynton, A. S.	*Echo*	Griffin, Ga.
Brinckley, A. W.	*Delaware Twilight*	Wilmington
Brown, J. E.	*Vindicator*	San Francisco, Calif.
Brown, W. C.	*Tribune*	Staunton, Va.
Buckner, R. J.	*People's Light*	Pulaski, Va.
Burnett, A. S.	*Avalanche*	Des Moines, Iowa
Cain, R. H.	*Missionary Record*	Charleston, S.C.
Caldwell, P.	*Standard Echo*	Philadelphia, Pa.
Carter, W. H.	*Times*	Sedalia, Mo.
Chacey, H. C.	*Wyandotte Echo*	Kans.
Cheeks, E. F.	*Cleveland Guide*	Ohio
Chiles, Nick	*Plaindealer*	Topeka, Kans.
Clark, F. R.	*New Jersey Record*	Newark
Clinton, John	*Reporter*	Richmond, Va.
Coffin, A./H. Judge Moore/Timothy Hurley/Richard H. Cain	*South Carolina Leader*	Charleston
Cole, O. Willis	*Louisville Leader*	Ky.
Coles, H. W.	*Rochester Voice*	N.Y.
Collins, M. L.	*Shreveport Sun*	La.
Conway, W. A.	*American Ethiopia*	Norfolk, Va.
Cooley, C. D.	*Caret*	Newport News, Va.
Cooley, C. D.	*Carolina Enterprise*	Goldsboro, N.C.
Coppin, L. J.	*Southwestern Christian Advocate*	Philadelphia, Pa.
Council, W. H.	*Huntsville Herald*	Ala.
Council, Wm. H.	*Negro Watchman*	Montgomery, Ala.
Cozart, W. Forrest	*Free Lance*	Chicago, Ill.
Crockett, Wm. F./T. A. Curtis	*Argus*	Montgomery, Ala.
Cromwell, R. I.	*Negro Gazette*	New Orleans, La.
Cromwell, J. W.	*People's Advocate*	Washington, D.C.
Dabney, W. P.	*Union*	Cincinnati, Ohio
Dalloz, C. J.	*La Tribune de La Nouvelle-Orleans*	La.
Davis, Almena	*Los Angeles Tribune*	Calif.
Davis, B. J.	*Independent*	Atlanta, Ga.
Davis, John H.	*Press*	Roanoke, Va.

Davis, S. B.	*Clipper*	Athens, Ga.
Davis, W. R.	*Republican*	New York, N.Y.
Day, W. H. H.	*The Alienated American*	Cleveland, Ohio
Dorman, P.	*Arkansas Survey*	Little Rock
Dorsey, C. Marcellus	*New Era*	Wilmington, Del.
Dorsey, Joseph	*Crusader*	Baltimore, Md.
Douglass, F.	*Frederick Douglass' Paper*	Rochester, N.Y.
Douglass, Lewis H./J. Seall Martin	*New National Era*	Washington, D.C.
Doyle, H. S.	*American Press*	Birmingham, Ala.
Duke, J. C.	*Echo*	Pine Bluff, Ark.
Duncan, J. T.	*Register*	San Antonio, Tex.
Dunjee, Roscoe	*Black Dispatch*	Oklahoma City, Okla.
Durr, Robert	*Birmingham Review*	Ala.
Duvall, C. V.	*Free Press*	Charleston, S.C.
Ellis, T. J.	*Delta News*	Mobile, Ala.
Fleming, J. L.	*Free Speech*	Chicago, Ill.
Fleming, Thomas C.	*San Francisco Reporter*	Calif.
Floyd, Silas Xavier	*Sentinel*	Augusta, Ga.
Flynn, R. A.	*National Negro Voice*	New Orleans, La.
Forte, O. A.	*Cleveland Herald*	Ohio
Franklin, C. A.	*Call*	Kansas City, Mo.
Frederick, Isaac	*Radical*	St. Joseph, Mo.
Frederick, N. J.	*Palmetto Leader*	Columbia, S.C.
Gay, Eustace	*Philadelphia Tribune*	Pa.
Gee, J. M.	*New Idea*	Selma, Ala.
Goff, Robert W.	*Interpreter*	Lynchburg, Va.
Gordon, A. A.	*Reporter*	Atlanta, Ga.
Grant, Rev. J. H.	*National Republican*	Greenville, Ga.
Griffin, J. M.	*Sunday Unionist*	Owensboro, Ky.
Hackley, Edwin H.	*Statesman*	Denver, Colo.
Hagler, H. A.	*Southern Age*	Atlanta, Ga.
Hamilton, Robert	*Weekly Anglo-African*	New York, N.Y.
Hamilton, West A.	*Sentinel*	Washington, D.C.
Harris, Edgar G.	*Illinois Times*	Champaign
Harvey, B. T.	*Columbus Messenger*	Ohio
Hatcher, H. H.	*Informer*	Louisville, Ky.
Haughton, Alfred	*Chronicle*	Boston, Mass.
Hawkins, Rev. S. T.	*Chronometer*	Americus, Ga.
Hendley, Charles, Jr.	*Huntsville Gazette*	Ala.
Hodges, Willis A./ Thomas Van Rensselaer	*Ram's Horn*	New York, N.Y.

Hoodes, S. I. R.	*Journal*	Pittsburgh, Pa.
Houston, H.	*Post*	Charlotte, N.C.
Howard, Charles P., Jr.	*Lake County Observer*	Gary, Ind.
Jackson, Allie W.	*Clarion*	Waco, Tex.
Jackson, Emory O.	*Birmingham World*	Ala.
Jackson, Giles B./W. S. Blackburn	*Negro Criterion*	Richmond, Va.
Jeltz, F. L.	*Kansas State Ledger*	Topeka
Jervay, P. R.	*Carolinian*	Raleigh, N.C.
Jervay, Thomas C.	*Wilmington Journal*	N.C.
Jessup, Landon/D. Betts Robinson	*Standard*	Norfolk, Va.
Johnson, Rev. Emanuel	*New Light*	Forrest City, Ark.
Johnson, P. H.	*The Laborer* [see *Laboring Man* in checklist]	Lynchburg, Va.
Johnson, Sol. C.	*Savannah Tribune*	Ga.
Johnson, W. H.	*Capitol*	Albany, N.Y.
Jolley, Levi	*Afro-American*	Philadelphia, Pa.
Jones, J. S.	*Searchlight*	Lake Charles, La.
Joseph, Philip	*Huntsville Gazette*	Ala.
Josey, J. Anthony	*Wisconsin Enterprise Blade*	Milwaukee
Kirkwood, O.	*Industrial Era*	Beaumont, Tex.
Lawrence, P.	*People's Choice*	Opelika, Ala.
Lawrence, Thomas A.	*Right House*	Ky.
Lenox, Cornelius	*Clipper*	Chicago, Ill.
Lewis, Matthew N.	*Newport News Star*	Va.
Lewis, Matthew N.	*Evening Recorder*	Newport News, Va.
Littlejohn, T. B.	*Progress*	Helena, Ark.
Lowe, E. W.	*Blade*	Eatonton, Ga.
McAden, R. G.	*Gleanor*	Madison, Ga.
McCall, J. E.	*Detroit Tribune*	Mich.
McCants, S. T.	*Northwest Herald*	Seattle, Wash.
McCollum, Obie	*Afro-American*	Richmond, Va.
McCray, John H.	*Lighthouse and Informer*	Columbia, S.C.
McGill, Rev. Wm.	*Metropolitan Journal*	Birmingham, Ala.
Mackey, A. B.	*Review*	Petersburg, Va.
Martin, L. E.	*Michigan Chronicle*	Detroit
Meine, C. F.	*Monitor*	New Orleans, La.
Miller, Loren	*Los Angeles Sentinel*	Calif.
Minton, E. D.	*Record*	Shreveport, La.
Mitchell, J. E.	*St. Louis Argus*	Mo.

Mooreland, Dr. Marc	*New Jersey Herald News*	Newark
Morris, James M./ Milton S. Malone	*Valley Index*	Staunton, Va.
Murphy, Carl	*Afro-American*	Baltimore, Md.
Murray, Jordon S.	*State Capital*	Springfield, Ill.
Murrell, Wm.	*New Jersey Trumpet*	Newark
Neal, G. A./F. Clark	*Broad Axe*	Pittsburgh, Pa.
Neal, Rev. J. F.	*Arkansas Baptist Flashlight*	Fort Smith
Newman, C. E.	*Minneapolis Spokesman*	Minn.
Newman, C. E.	*St. Paul Recorder*	Minn.
Newman, W.	*People's Defender*	Jackson, Miss.
Newsome, J. Thomas	*Newport News Star*	Va.
Oldfield, J. J. J.	*Defender*	Chattanooga, Tenn.
Parr, U. S.	*Baptist Vanguard*	Little Rock, Ark.
Penn, J. A.	*Laboring Man*	Lynchburg, Va.
Phillips, T. H.	*Western Optic*	Moberly, Mo.
Pledger, W. A.	*Age*	Atlanta, Ga.
Pope, W. M.	*Call*	Topeka, Kans.
Potter, M. D.	*Tampa Bulletin*	Fla.
Porter, Webster L.	*East Tennessee News*	Knoxville
Powell, C. B.	*Amsterdam News*	New York, N.Y.
Pratt, George R.	*Press*	Port Royal, Va.
Presnell, Dr. J. H.	*Herald*	Knoxville, Tenn.
Putnam, Louis M.	*The Colored Man's Journal*	New York, N.Y.
Quo, E. H.	*Plain-Dealer*	Valdosta, Ga.
Ralph, S. H.	*Watchman*	Shreveport, La.
Randolph, B. F./E. S. Adams Sones	*Charlestown Journal*	S.C.
Rawlings, T. P.	*All About Us*	Chicago, Ill.
Reeves, H. E. S.	*Miami Times*	Fla.
Rhone, L. J.	*Messenger*	Waco, Tex.
Rice, C. W.	*Negro Labor News*	Houston, Tex.
Rives, John H.	*Forum*	Dayton, Ohio
Robinson, D. L.	*Tribune*	Wichita, Kans.
Robinson, M. L.	*Leader*	Alexandria, Va.
Robinson, Wm. J.	*Independent*	Detroit, Mich.
Rogers, F. L.	*Illinois Conservator*	Springfield
Rogers, W. H.	*Light*	Vicksburg, Miss.
Russw[u]rm, John/ Samuel Cornish	*Freedom's Journal*	New York, N.Y.
Ruffin, R. I.	*Southern Sentinel*	Ala.

Sella, John/P. S. B. Pinchback	*The Louisianian Daily*	New Orleans
Scott, C. A.	*Atlanta Daily World*	Ga.
Scott, D. A.	*Texas Headlight*	Austin
Scott, George W.	*Arkansas Survey-Journal*	Little Rock
Scott, Napoleon, Jr.	*Muskogee Lantern*	Okla.
Scott, W. S.	*The Cairo Gazette*	Ill.
Severns, Jeanne	*Criterion*	Los Angeles, Calif.
Seymour, M. O.	*Western Ideal*	Pueblo, Colo.
Shields, A. G., Jr.	*Arkansas World*	Little Rock
Simms & Gould	*Rescue*	New Orleans, La.
Smith, B. Branner	*Flashlight Herald*	Knoxville, Tenn.
Smith, H. C.	*Southern American*	Chattanooga, Tenn.
Smith, J. Robert	*Tri-County Bulletin*	San Bernardino, Calif.
Smith, Rev. T. N. M.	*Southern News*	Savannah, Ga.
Smith, Wm. M.	*Echo*	Beaumont, Tex.
Soloman, Sam B.	*Miami Whip*	Fla.
Stamps, T. B.	*Vindicator*	New Orleans, La.
Stanley, Frank L.	*Louisville Defender*	Ky.
Stewart, Marcus	*Indianapolis Recorder*	Ind.
Street, J. Gordon	*Boston Courant*	Mass.
Sweets, N. A.	*St. Louis American*	Mo.
Swingler, L. O.	*Memphis World*	Tenn.
Sylvahn, J. Luther	*Progressive Herald*	Syracuse, N.Y.
Taylor, Rev. R. M. S.	*Afro-American Mouthpiece*	Valdosta, Ga.
Thomas, W. H.	*Signal*	Cumberland, Md.
Thomason, G. M.	*Herald*	Forrest City, Ark.
Toussaint, A. J.	*Progressive Age*	Alexandria, La.
Trotter, Wm. Monroe	*Guardian*	Boston, Mass.
Turner, J. Thomas	*Watchman*	Memphis, Tenn.
Van Pelt, L. J.	*Arkansas Appreciator*	Fort Smith
Vaughan, Benjamin F./ Wallace Van Jackson	*Voice*	Richmond, Va.
Walker, Wm. O.	*Cleveland Call and Post*	Ohio
Washington, F. E.	*Colored Citizen*	Pensacola, Fla.
Wheeler, J. W.	*Palladium*	St. Louis, Mo.
White, Albert S.	*New South*	Louisville, Ky.
Williams, Dr. E. A.	*Ferret and Journal of the Lodge*	New Orleans, La.
Williams, George N.	*Commoner*	Washington, D.C.
Williams, John Albert	*Omaha Monitor*	Nebr.
Williams, Milton G.	*Twin City Observer*	Minneapolis, Minn.
Willis, Ellis	*Item*	Dallas, Tex.
Wilson, Joseph T.	*Industrial Day*	Richmond, Va.

Wood, Scott	*Herald*	Petersburg, Va.
Wright, G. H.	*Register*	Hannibal, Mo.
Young, P. B., Sr.	*Journal and Guide*	Norfolk, Va.
Young, James H.	*Gazette*	Raleigh, N.C.

Copublishers (locate by main listing, which follows)

Adams Sones, E. S./Randolph, B. F.
Blackburn, W. S./Jackson, Giles B.
Bush, R. O./Bowley, Peter
Cain, Richard H./Coffin, A. (also independent)
Clark, F./Neal, G. A.
Cornish, Samuel/Russw[u]rm, John
Curtis, T. A./Crockett, Wm. F.
Gould/Simms
Hurley, Timothy/Coffin, A.
Jackson, Wallace Van/Vaughan, Benjamin F.
Johnson, P. H./J.A. Penn
Malone, Milton S./Morris, James M.
Martin, J. Seall/Douglass, Lewis H.
Moore, H. Judge/Coffin, A.
Newsome, J. Thomas/Lewis, Matthew N.
Pinchback, P. S. B./Sella, John
Robinson, D. Betts/Jessup, Landon
Van Rensselaer, Thomas/Hodges, Willis A.

SUPPLEMENTARY LISTS

Warren H. Brown's Checklist of Negro Weekly Newspapers, 1827–1880

This list of weekly newspapers reveals Brown's interest in the black press for (probably) more than a decade. It is the seed of the idea he went back to after the disastrous essay of 1942–1943. It is this list, from his Ph.D. dissertation (1941, 159–166), on which Brown built his major checklist.

The Advance	[Montgomery,] Ala.
American Citizen	[Baltimore,] Md.
Arkansas Dispatch (*The Mansion*)	[Little Rock]
Arkansas Freeman	[Little Rock]

The Athens Blade	Ga.
Black Republican	[New Orleans,] La.
The Bulletin	[Louisville,] Ky.
Charlest[o]n Journal	S.C.
Colored American	[Augustus,] Ga.
The Colored American	[New York,] N.Y.
Colored Citizen	[Cincinnati,] Ohio
Colored Citizen	[Topeka/Wichita, ??] Kans.
The Colored Tennessean	[Nashville]
The Elevator	[San Francisco,] Calif.
Frederick Douglass' Paper (North Star)	[Rochester,] N.Y.
Freedom's Journal Rights of All	[New York,] N.Y.
The Free Press	[Charleston,] S.C.
Georgetown Planet Weekly	S.C.
Huntsville Gazette	Ala.
Loyal Georgian	[Augusta,] Ga.
Missionary Record	[Charleston,] S.C.
Negro Gazette	[New Orleans,] La.
The New National Era	[Washington,] D.C.
New Orleans Semi-Weekly Louisianian	La.
New Orleans Weekly Louisianian	La.
People's Advocate	[Washington,] D.C.
Savannah Weekly Echo	Ga.
South Carolina Leader	[Charleston,] S.C.
Topeka Tribune	Kans.
L'Union	[New Orleans,] La.
Virginia Star	[Richmond]
Weekly Anglo-African	[New York,] N.Y.
The Weekly Defiance	[Atlanta,] Ga.
The Weekly Loyal Georgian	[?] Ga.

Editors Listed by George Gore, Jr.

Allen, William G.	*National Watchman and Clarion*	Troy, N.Y.	1842
Alexander, W. M.	*The Afro-American*	Baltimore, Md.	1893
Bell, Phillip	*The Elevator*	Albany, N.Y.	1842
Carter, W. H.	*Mirror of the Times*	San Francisco, Calif.	1855
Chase, William	*The Washington Bee*	D.C.	1882
Clark, Peter	*Herald of Freedom*	?, Ohio	1855

Clarke, M. M.	Christian Recorder*	Philadelphia, Pa.	1852
	[Originally The Mystery, then The Christian Herald]	[Pittsburgh, Pa.]	[1842/1848]
Cooper, Edw., and Knox, Geo.	Indianapolis Freeman	Ind.	1884
Delany, Martin	The Mystery*	Pittsburgh, Pa.	1848
Fortune, T. T.	New York Age	N.Y.	1888
Freeman, John J.	The Progressive American	New York, N.Y.	1861
Gibbs, Judge	Mirror of the Times (Later Pacific Appeal 1862)	San Francisco, Calif.	1855
Hamilton, Thomas	People's Press	New York, N.Y.	1843
Mitchell, John	Richmond Planet	Va.	1884
Perry, Christopher	Philadelphia Tribune	Pa.	1881
Sampson, John P.	The Colored Citizen	Cincinnati, Ohio	1863
Shuften, J. T.	The Colored American	August[a], Ga.	1865
Smith, H. C.	Cleveland Gazette	Ohio	1883
Spellman, James, J., and Lynch, John	The Colored Citizen	Miss.	1870
Weaver, Elisha	Christian Recorder*	Philadelphia, Pa.	1861
Wright, R. R., Jr.	Christian Recorder*	Philadelphia, Pa.	1922

---

*"In 1848 the African Methodist Episcopal Church purchased the Mystery of Pittsburgh, Pa., of which Martin Delaney [sic] was editor. During the four years of its existence in Pittsburgh, the paper was known as the Christian Herald. In 1852, the paper was moved to Philadelphia, and its name was changed to Christian Recorder. Rev. M. M. Clarke became its first editor.

"The beginning of the Christian Recorder in 1852 marks the founding of the oldest Negro newspaper in existence today. . . . The early years were beset with many difficulties, and oftimes the paper was not issued regularly. Not until Elisha Weaver became editor in 1861 did it appear weekly" (Gore, 8). In 1922, its editor was R. R. Wright, Jr.

Additional Antebellum Newspapers Listed by George Gore, Jr.

The papers listed here appear on the lists of Martin Delany (MD) and/or Martin Dann (D).

1842	*The Elevator* (MD)	Albany, N.Y.
1842	*The Mystery* (MD, D)	Pittsburgh, Pa.
1842	*National Watchman and Clarion* (MD, D)	Troy, N.Y.
1843	*The People's Press* (D)	New York, N.Y.
1848	*The Christian Herald* (Formerly *The Mystery*) (D)	Pittsburgh, Pa.
1848	*The Impartial Citizen* (MD)	Syracuse, N.Y.
1855	*Herald of Freedom* (D)	[?,] Ohio
1855	*Mirror of the Times* (First West Coast paper) (D)	San Francisco, Calif.

REFERENCES

Brooks, Maxwell R. *The Negro Press Re-Examined*. Boston: Christopher Publishing House, 1959.

Brown, Warren Henry. "Social Change and the Negro Press 1860–1880." Ph.D. dissertation, New School for Social Research, 1941, 166 pp.

_____. "A Negro Looks at the Negro Press." *Saturday Review of Literature* 25(19 Dec. 1942):5–6.

_____. "A Negro Warns the Negro Press." *Reader's Digest* 42(Jan. 1943):32–34.

_____. "Con: The Case Against the Negro Press." *Negro Digest* 1(Feb. 1943):44–46.

_____. *Checklist of Negro Newspapers in the United States (1872–1946)*. Lincoln University Journalism Series No. 2. Jefferson City, Mo.: Lincoln University, 1946.

Cayton, Horace R., and St. Clair Drake. *Black Metropolis*. New York: Harcourt, Brace & Co., 1945.

Cunard, Nancy. "Harlem Reviewed." In *Negro, an Anthology*. Ed. Nancy Cunard, 67–74. London: Wishart, 1934.

Dann, Martin E. *The Black Press 1827–1890*. New York: Putnam, 1971.

Delany, Martin. *Condition, Elevation, Emigration, and Destiny of the Colored People of the United States Politically Considered*. Philadelphia: Author, 1852. Reprint, New York: Arno Press, 1968.

Detweiler, Frederick G. *The Negro Press in the United States*. Chicago: University of Chicago Press, 1922. Reprint, College Park, Md.: McGrath, 1968.

_____. "The Negro Press Today." *American Journal of Sociology* 44, No. 3(1938):391–401.

Finkle, Lee. *Forum for Protest: The Black Press During World War II*. Cranbury, N.J.: Associated University Presses, 1975.

Forten, Charlotte. *The Journal of Charlotte Forten*. Ed. Ray Allen Billington. New York: W. W. Norton, 1953/1981.

Franklin, John Hope. *From Slavery to Freedom*. New York: Knopf, 1947; 3d ed. 1967.

Gore, George, Jr. *Negro Journalism: An Essay on the History and Present Condition of the Negro Press*. Greencastle, Ind.: DePauw University, 1922.

Gwaltney, John L. *Drylongso*. New York: Random House, 1980.

Haley, James T. *Sparkling Gems of Race Knowledge Worth Reading*. Compiled and arranged by James T. Haley. Nashville, Tenn.: J. T. Haley & Co., 1897.

Harper, Frances Ellen Watkins. *A Brighter Coming Day: A France Ellen Watkins Harper Reader*. Ed. Frances Smith Foster. New York: CUNY Feminist Press, 1990.

Kerlin, Robert T. *The Voice of the Negro, 1919.* New York: E. P. Dutton, 1920. Reprint, New York: Arno Press, 1968.

Kirby, John B. *Black Americans in the Roosevelt Era: Liberalism and Race.* Knoxville: University of Tennessee Press, 1980.

LaBrie, Henry G. III. *Perspectives of the Black Press: 1974.* Kennebunkport, Maine: Mercer House, 1974.

"Letters of Negro Migrants of 1916–1918." *Journal of Negro History* 4(July and Oct. 1919):290–340, 412–65. Collected under the direction of Emmett J. Scott.

Mossell, Mrs. N. F. *The Work of the Afro-American Woman.* 1894. Reprint ed. Joanne Braxton. New York: Oxford, 1988.

Oak, Vishnu V. "What About the Negro Press?" *Saturday Review of Literature* 26(6 Mar. 1943):4–5.

Penn, I. Garland. *The Afro-American Press and Its Editors.* Springfield, Mass.: Willey and Co., 1890, 1891. Facsimile reprints, New York: Arno Press, 1969; Salem, N.H.: Ayer Company, Publishers, 1988.

Pride, Armistead Scott. "A Register and History of Negro Newspapers in the United States: 1827–1950." Ph.D. dissertation, Northwestern University, 1950, 426 pp. University Microfilms (Xerox), Ann Arbor, Mich.

Schomburg Center for Research in Black Culture. *Freedom's Journals: A History of the Black Press in New York State.* New York: N.Y. Public Library, 1986.

Spillers, Hortense. "A Hateful Passion, a Lost Love." *Feminist Issues in Literary Scholarship.* Ed. S. Benstock. Bloomington: Indiana University Press, 1987.

Taylor, Susie King. "Reminiscences of my life in camp" (1902). In *Black Writers and the American Civil War.* Ed. Richard A. Long. Secaucus, N.J.: The Blue & Grey Press, 1988.

Wells-Barnett, Ida B. *Crusade for Justice: The Autobiography of Ida B. Wells.* Ed. Alfreda M. Duster. Chicago: University of Chicago Press, 1970.

———. *Southern Horrors. Lynch Law in All Its Phases* (1892). New Hampshire: Ayer, 1987.

Wolseley, Roland E. *The Black Press, U.S.A.* Ames: Iowa State University Press, 1971.